SEP 3 '87	DATE DUE	
APR 8 '88		
APR 02 '97		
MAR 2 3 2020		

VISUAL SCIENCE
MICROBES

Jim Teasdale

Silver Burdett Company

Editor Margaret Conroy
Design Richard Garratt
Consultant Zbigniew Towalski
Picture Research Caroline Mitchell
Production Susan Mead
Text research Julie Rees
and John Watkins

A MACDONALD BOOK

First published in Great Britain in 1984
by Macdonald & Co. (Publishers) Ltd
London & Sydney

Adapted and published
in the United States
by Silver Burdett Company
Morristown, N.J.

1985 Printing

ISBN 0-382-06835-1 (Lib. Bdg.)
ISBN 0-382-09002-0

Library of Congress
Catalog Card Number 84-50818

Cover: Budding yeast

Right: Brew kettles

Contents

What are microbes?

Microbes are living things which are so small that they can only be seen clearly by using a microscope. They are a large and varied group that exist as single cells or collections of cells. (A cell is the smallest unit of life.) Each cell of a microbe can live independently of other cells. All of the processes of life can take place inside one cell. Human bodies are made of millions of cells and different types of cell have different functions. If we took one cell from our bodies it could not survive on its own. Each different type needs to be with other cells in order to be able to live.

Where are they found? What do they do?

Most microbes are useful and not harmful. Microbes are the simplest forms of life on Earth and there are more microbes on or in one human body than there are people on Earth. These numerous microbes cannot all be harm-

ful, otherwise we would all have diseases all of the time. Their presence is essential to our health, in fact.

Microbes can be found everywhere on Earth. They live and grow in hot springs and arctic wastes. They are even present in the radiators and pipes of central heating systems. Microbes are used to make many of our foods, to fertilize our soils, to make useful chemicals, to clean our water supplies and to get rid of our waste materials. Some microbes may cause diseases of plants or animals, but drugs and vaccines can now be made to combat most diseases. These drugs and vaccines are often made by microbes.

Microbes are used world-wide in industry to make many useful products. If you eat bread, butter, cheese or yoghurt, put vinegar on your chips or wash your clothes with biological washing powders then you are using some of these microbial products. Microbes

have been used in bread-making for thousands of years, but now scientists are finding many new uses for microbes.

Groups of microbes

There are five main groups of microbes. The smallest are viruses. Some of these cause common diseases such as colds and 'flu. Viruses must enter other living cells before they become active and make more viruses. Bacteria are also very small and usually consist of only one cell. Many types of bacteria are used in cheese-making.

Algae are simple plants which live in water and have no stems, roots or leaves. The green slime in a stagnant pond is algae growing there. Fungi are non-green organisms which cannot make their own food. Yeast, used in bread-making, is a fungus. Some algae and fungi may be seen without a microscope when they form large groups of several cells.

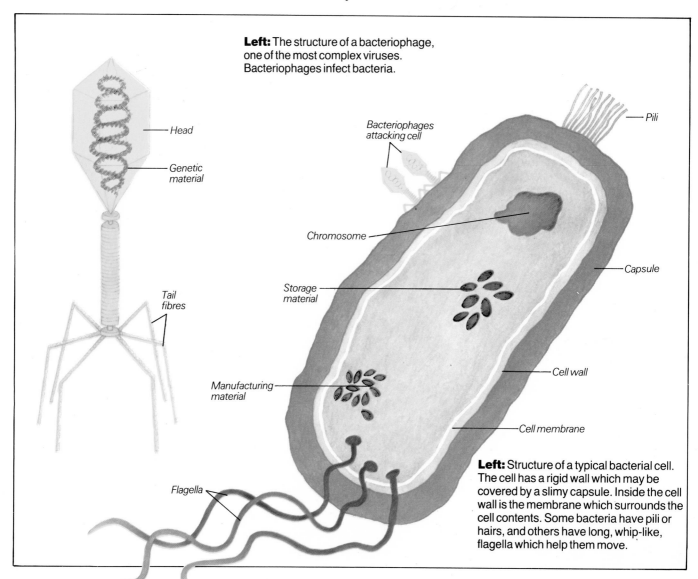

Left: The structure of a bacteriophage, one of the most complex viruses. Bacteriophages infect bacteria.

Head

Genetic material

Tail fibres

Bacteriophages attacking cell

Pili

Chromosome

Storage material

Capsule

Manufacturing material

Cell wall

Cell membrane

Flagella

Left: Structure of a typical bacterial cell. The cell has a rigid wall which may be covered by a slimy capsule. Inside the cell wall is the membrane which surrounds the cell contents. Some bacteria have pili or hairs, and others have long, whip-like, flagella which help them move.

Protozoans are single-celled animals. They live in water or where it is damp. The disease malaria is caused by a protozoan which is injected into the human body by a mosquito.

Microbes are regarded by most scientists as being a distinct group of living organisms, separate from plants and animals. Some microbes such as algae can be classified as plants, and protozoans as animals, but both can also be grouped with other microbes because of their structure and the way they live.

Microbes are so small that almost nothing was known about them until the first microscope was invented. But people had been using them long before that, to make bread, cheese, wine and beer.

Below: A cluster of diatoms in a water sample. Diatoms are single-celled algae.

Bottom: The growth of microbes on an agar plate which has been exposed to air for a few minutes.

Above: Filaments of the alga *Spirogyra*. Cells are joined end to end to make up the filaments. The chloroplasts, which contain the green pigment of the cells, have a spiral structure.

Below: A fungus fairy ring. The underground threads or hyphae of the fungus grow outwards from a central point and so the fruiting bodies (mushrooms) appear in a ring. The fairy ring releases food which improves the growth of grass on each side of it.

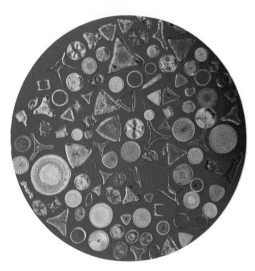

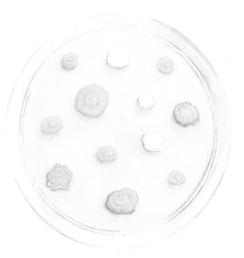

Improved growth of grass

Grass between mushrooms is poorer because of fungal hyphae clogging roots

Seeing microbes

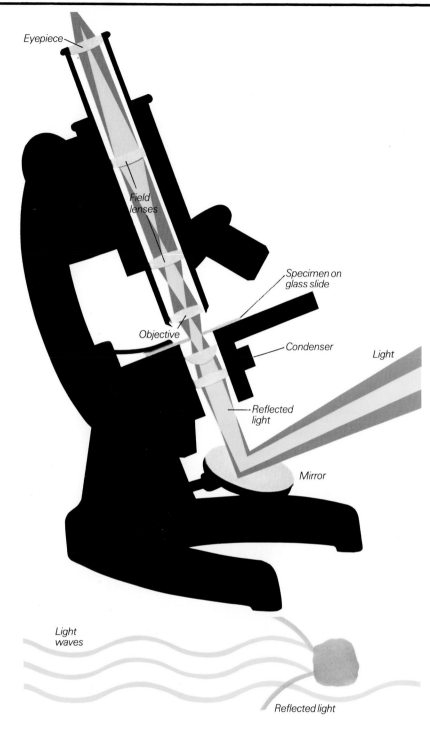

Eyepiece

Field lenses

Specimen on glass slide

Objective

Condenser

Light

Reflected light

Mirror

Light waves

Reflected light

Many of the major advances that have occurred in biology during the last 200 years have been due to the development and improvement of the microscope. Lenses as magnifiers have a long history. Burning glasses were known to the ancient Egyptians. An Arab in about AD 1020 correctly realized that it was the convex shape of a lens which made it able to enlarge objects. You have probably used a convex-shaped lens in a magnifying glass.

The first microscope

The majority of microbes are very small and transparent and cannot be seen by using a magnifying glass. They were not discovered until the last half of the 17th century when Anton van Leeuwenhoek, a Dutchman, whose hobby was making lenses, made one of the first microscopes. This could magnify up to about 200 times. Leeuwenhoek examined things such as soil and milk and was able to see a whole new world of tiny living creatures which no-one had dreamed of before. He called these minute creatures 'animalcules' or little animals. Today we call them microbes.

A modern microscope

You will probably use a microscope in school. Like the one developed by Leeuwenhoek, your school microscope uses light and glass lenses to magnify objects. There are two lenses in most school microscopes, which will magnify objects about 400 times. If one lens magnifies by 20 times, the object being examined appears to be 20 times larger. If a second lens (which itself magnifies 20 times) is correctly lined up with the first, then the object will appear 400 times (20 × 20) larger.

In order to let light through, the object needs to be very thin and is placed on a transparent glass slide. Sometimes the object is stained or coloured with dye so that it can be seen clearly. However, even by using a good light microscope which can magnify more than 400 times, the detailed structure of many microbes cannot be seen clearly.

Left, above: A light microscope. The wavelength diagram shows that only a few waves of light hit a tiny object and are reflected.

Left: Bacteria magnified 500 times by a light microscope.

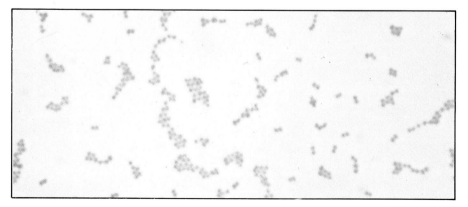

Sizes and shapes of microbes

The size of microbial cells is usually measured in micrometres (abbreviated to μm). There are 1000 μm in one millimetre, so one micrometre equals one thousandth of a millimetre. Viruses are usually less than 1 μm in size, whereas most bacteria are between 1 and 10 μm in size.

To give you an idea of how small bacteria are, if 2000 'typical' bacteria were placed close together they would only cover the head of a pin. Under a powerful light microscope, bacterial cells can be recognized by their shape. There are three main shapes: round, rod-shaped and spiral-shaped.

Most fungi are large compared to bacteria because they are made up of long threads or hyphae. These often produce a visible, fluffy mass – such as mould growing on old bread. Some hyphae develop 'fruiting bodies' – mushrooms or toadstools.

Algae vary in size and shape. Some algae are single-celled and microscopic but others are made up of a ball of cells and others of cells making up strands or filaments.

Some protozoans, such as amoeba, have a shape that changes whereas others have a fixed shape. For example, paramecium is slipper-shaped. Amoeba can be up to 150 μm across.

The electron microscope

In 1932 the electron microscope was invented. It uses beams of electrons instead of light rays. The use of electrons improves the magnifying power so that much smaller objects, even the insides of microbes, can be seen clearly. Some electron microscopes magnify up to a million times.

The lenses in an electron microscope are not made of glass, but of coils of wire with electric currents running through them. This causes a magnetic field to be produced which focuses the beam of electrons.

Microbes, including viruses, can be seen in detail by using electron microscopes, but they are very large and expensive pieces of equipment.

Right, above: An electron microscope. The wavelength diagram shows how more electrons hit a tiny object and so they give a better image.

Right: Bacteria magnified 20500 times by an electron microscope.

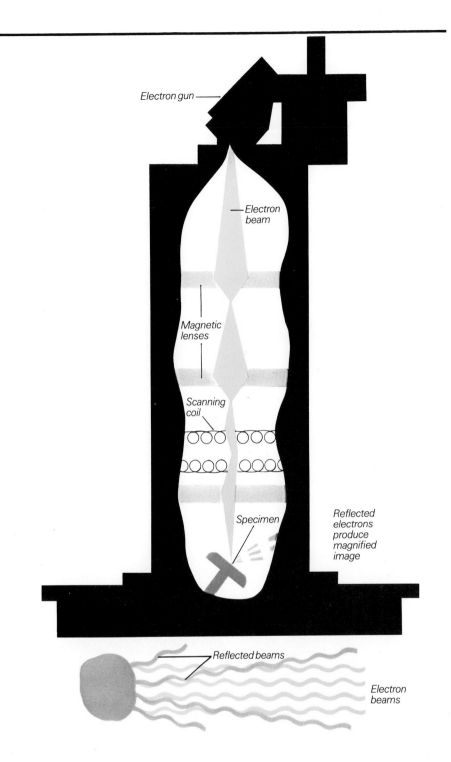

Electron gun

Electron beam

Magnetic lenses

Scanning coil

Specimen

Reflected electrons produce magnified image

Reflected beams

Electron beams

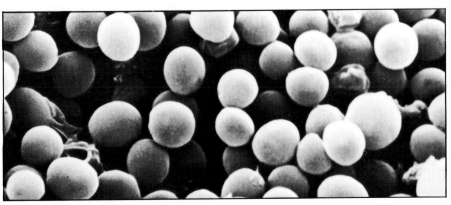

How microbes work

All of the activities of life occur inside the cells of most microbes. These activities include feeding, respiring and reproducing. Microbes have many different ways of carrying out these processes. Viruses, however, do not respire or feed and can only 'live' in other living cells. Viruses do not die if they are not inside other living cells but they are inactive.

Below: Yeasts divide by producing buds which grow bigger and may break away from the parent cell. This picture is taken through a light microscope.

Bottom: Budding yeast cells magnified 3900 times by an electron microscope.

Feeding

Like all green plants, algae can make their own food (as do some bacteria). They combine together carbon dioxide – a gas in the air – with water as they trap sunlight energy. This is the process of photosynthesis which produces food and gives off the gas oxygen as a by-product. You may have noticed bubbles of this gas near pond weeds when the sun is shining.

Fungi do not contain the green chlorophyll which is essential for photosynthesis, so cannot make their own food. Some live on the dead remains of plants and animals and cause decay. Some bacteria feed in a similar way. The decay process breaks down the dead bodies of animals and plants and returns vital minerals to the soil.

Other bacteria and fungi live on or in the bodies of plants and animals. These types cause disease. Athlete's foot is a common disease of the feet which is caused by a fungus. You don't have to be an athlete to catch this disease! The fungus thrives in damp, warm conditions and so lives between the toes where it irritates the skin and causes cracks.

The protozoa are animals and like all animals need a ready-made food supply. They may move around in order to catch their food. Look at a drop of pond water under a microscope and you will see lots of these animals darting around in all directions.

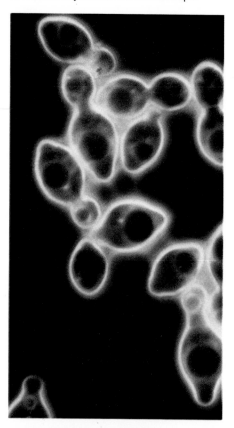

Above: Algal growth on a canal. This is a common sight on still water such as ponds and canals. Bubbles of oxygen can be seen around the green algae.

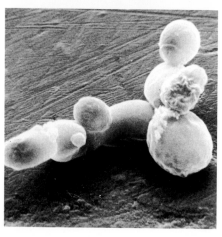

Below: Fly mould growing around a dead house fly. As the mould feeds on the body, it gradually causes decay of the remains.

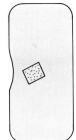

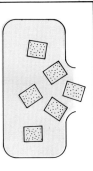

Above: Viral reproduction. The virus passes through the cell membrane of the cell it is attacking.

Above: The contents of the virus are released into the cell. The virus takes control of the cell.

Above: The cell is used to produce many copies of the virus. Once they are complete, they are released to attack other cells.

Respiration

Microbes must change the food that they have obtained into energy to keep them alive. This process is called respiration and as well as releasing energy, it also produces the gas carbon dioxide as a waste product.

There are two types of respiration – one using oxygen, the other without. Like ourselves, many microbes need oxygen from the air to convert their food into energy. However, some microbes can respire without oxygen. Yeasts respire without oxygen during the production of wine and beer.

Reproduction

If life is to continue from one generation to the next then living things must reproduce. There are two ways in which microbes can reproduce. The simplest method is asexual – it involves just a single microbe which divides to produce two small, identical versions of itself. Under good conditions this can occur once every 20 minutes, so that if we start with one microbe we have two after 20 minutes. This can be a very rapid means of reproduction and many new cells can be made in a short time.

The other method is called sexual re-production and requires two parents. Their reproductive cells join together to produce one new cell which carries some characteristics of each parent and is not identical to either of them.

Viruses cannot reproduce by themselves. They invade and enter other plant, animal or microbe cells, causing changes and often damage. They take over the cells and can produce copies of themselves in a short time.

Below: Sexual reproduction in the alga, *Spirogyra*. The cell contents of two cells fuse.

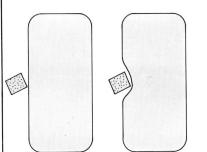

Below: Stages in bacterial division. The chromosomes divide before the cells do. In good conditions, the cells keep doubling their number.

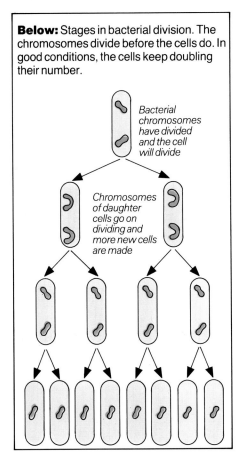

Bacterial chromosomes have divided and the cell will divide

Chromosomes of daughter cells go on dividing and more new cells are made

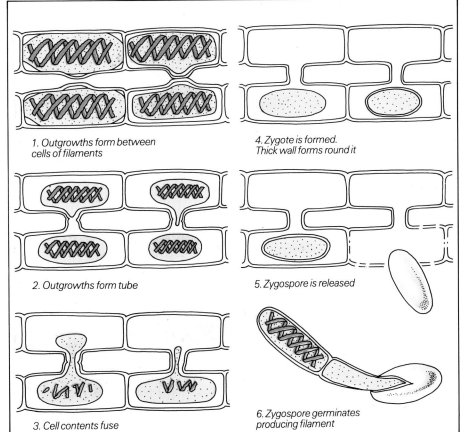

1. Outgrowths form between cells of filaments

2. Outgrowths form tube

3. Cell contents fuse

4. Zygote is formed. Thick wall forms round it

5. Zygospore is released

6. Zygospore germinates producing filament

9

Microbes, plants and animals

Above: Soil fungi called mycorrhizae extend the root systems of plants. The white mass above is formed by the mycorrhizae which help the plant to collect more water and food from a bigger soil area.

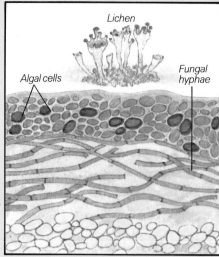

Above: A lichen and a cross-section showing its structure. The top layer consists of closely-packed fungal strands with green algal cells amongst them. Below this are more layers of fungal hyphae.

Most microbes, apart from algae, depend on other living things for their food. In some cases microbes live within other living things and cause harm, sometimes disease, when they feed there. The microbes are then said to be parasites. However, some microbes live together with other living things in such a way that no harm is caused. In fact, both partners can benefit from the relationship; for example, by improving each other's food supply. When two different kinds of organism live together and both benefit, the process is called symbiosis. The partners are symbionts.

Microbes can form such partnerships with other microbes or with plants or with animals.

Lichens

You have probably seen small, crusty plants growing on old stone walls, gravestones or roofs of cottages. These are lichens, which are formed by a partnership between a fungus and algal cells. They are able to grow in cold, exposed, dry positions where other plants cannot survive. It is for this reason that they are common in the Arctic and on rocky mountains. You may also have

seen lichens growing on the bark of trees or even on pebbles on the seashore.

The fungus in a lichen partnership cannot survive by itself. The algal cells can grow by themselves, but not as well as when they are with the fungus. The fungus and the algal cells must both benefit by living together as partners. The algal cells produce food which the fungus can use and the fungus improves the water supply to the alga and gives it shelter.

Lichens vary widely in appearance. They may be flat, leafy or bushy. In very polluted areas lichens cannot survive – there is a lichen desert. Flat lichens can grow where there is some pollution of the air, leafy lichens where there is less air pollution and bushy lichens where the air is pure. You only find bushy lichens in country areas well away from industrial smoke. Lichens can therefore be used as indicators of air pollution. By looking at the form of the lichens in an area you can tell if the air is polluted or clean. The bushier the lichens are, the purer the air is. Have a close look at old stone walls or the bark of trees in your area and estimate how clean the air is where you live.

Grass eaters

Animals such as rabbits and cows feed on grass. This contains a lot of a substance called cellulose, which these animals cannot break down or digest by themselves. They rely on microbes to do the job for them.

In the case of rabbits, bacteria live in a special part of the intestine called the caecum. The bacteria benefit as they

Above: Bacteria in a cow's rumen help digest grass. It is first stored in the rumen, one of the four compartments of the stomach.

Above: The grass is regurgitated into the mouth as cud to be ground into smaller pieces by chewing.

Above: Lichens can be used as indicators of pollution. Here, the prevailing winds blow smoke to the right and trees there have flat lichens on their trunks. Trees in less polluted areas have bushier lichens. In very polluted areas, no lichens will grow.

have a constant food supply. The rabbit benefits as cellulose in its food is broken down into sugars for energy.

'Germ-free' animals are sometimes reared under special laboratory conditions. Germ-free rabbits have a very large caecum which cannot work properly because there are no bacteria present in it. If they are given normal food, containing bacteria, the usual activity of the caecum is restored. These animals therefore rely on bacteria to survive in the wild.

Cows also have bacteria living in the part of their stomachs called the rumen. These bacteria also break down cellulose in the grass which the cow eats. It is possible that bacteria are also involved in the conversion of grass into milk. We could consider the cow to be a living, moving fermenter, a fermenter being a large vessel where bacteria multiply, respiring without oxygen, and make useful products.

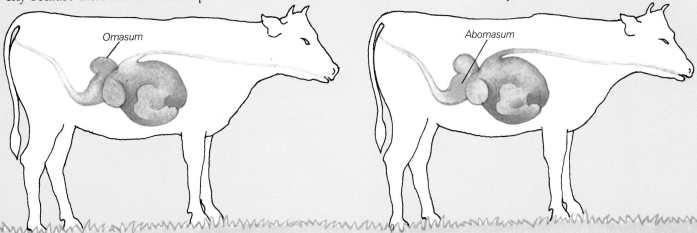

Above: The finely ground grass passes back into another compartment, the omasum, where water is absorbed.

Above: The final stages of digestion take place in the abomasum. Protein from dead microbes from the rumen is also digested.

Microbes and safety

If you leave bread in the bread bin for more than a week it will probably have fluffy mould growing on it. The same happens with old cheese. How does this happen? Microbes are everywhere. They are in the air, in soil, on food and on your body. Microbes multiply very quickly, especially where it is warm and damp. In the case of the old bread or cheese, fungal spores have settled from the air and started to grow hyphae on the food.

There are millions of microbes in the air. They settle like dust and if they land where conditions are suitable for growth then they multiply quickly. Moulds may not be harmful, but some are, and so are many other microbes. We must take care to make sure that microbes do not multiply and become a possible danger in areas where we do not want them.

Below: Kitchen hygiene prevents disease.

Microbes and the home

The simplest way to keep down the number of microbes is to keep yourself and your home clean. Microbes need food, moisture and a suitable temperature to grow and if any one of these conditions is not right then their growth will be restricted.

You must wash your hands after going to the lavatory and before eating or handling food. Knives, forks, other cutlery and cooking utensils should be kept clean. Work surfaces must be regularly washed with hot, clean, soapy water. Bathrooms and toilets are often warm and damp. Good ventilation helps keep them dry. They should be cleaned regularly using hot water and disinfectants. A disinfectant is a strong chemical which kills microbes.

Microbes and food

Food for us is food for microbes. If we like to eat it so do they. If warm food is left exposed to the air, microbes will settle on it and multiply quickly so that when the food is eaten harmful microbes may enter your body. For that reason it is best to cover food and keep it stored in a cool place.

Microbes can cause decay of food. This happens if you leave fruit for too long in the fruit bowl. Much of the pre-packed food we eat nowadays has been treated to prevent microbes from growing. Dried food, such as packet soups, contains no water so that microbes cannot multiply in it. Frozen food is kept at very low temperatures (-20°C), which do not kill the microbes, but do prevent them from reproducing rapidly. Tinned food is cooked at high temperatures which kill microbes. The food is canned and the tins sealed while the food is still hot so that there is little or no air present. This reduces the chance of any surviving microbes reproducing. Many foods have preservatives added to prevent microbes growing. A high sugar concentration prevents microbes from growing, and so fruit is often preserved in syrup or as jam.

Milk is a common food which is treated to remove microbes before it is sold to us. Three common types of milk nowadays are pasteurized, sterilized and Ultra Heat Treated (UHT) milk. Pasteurized milk is heated for a short time and then rapidly cooled. The heating kills some, but not all, microbes. Sterilized milk is heated to higher temperatures for a longer period of time so that all microbes are killed. UHT milk is heated to even higher temperatures, but for a short time only. Again all microbes are killed. The higher temperatures make the sugar in the milk 'caramelize' (like the sugar in toffee) and so affect the taste of the milk.

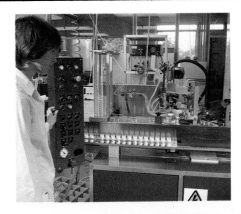

Left: Testing milk to make sure that the number of bacteria present is within defined limits. Milk can be contaminated if a cow is unhealthy or if a farmer is not following the correct procedures for hygienic milk production.

Below: Good hygiene is essential in hospitals where microbes could easily be passed from one patient to another. Here, sterilized equipment is being put out ready for an operation.

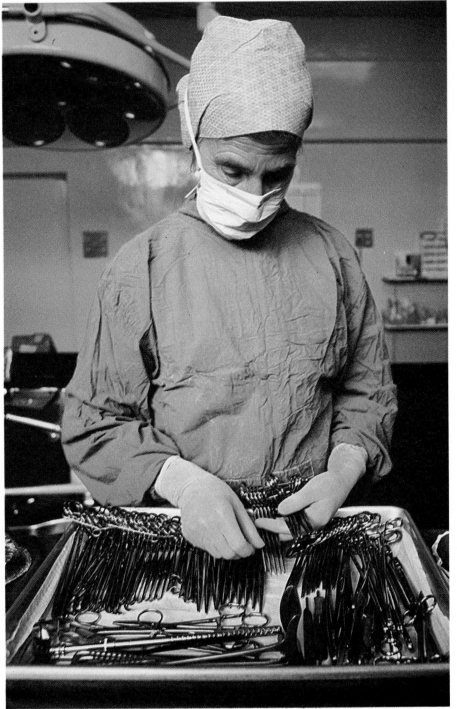

Tests are carried out on milk before it is sold to make sure that microbes are not present. Sterilized milk and UHT milk will keep for a long time (even in a fairly warm place) if they are kept sealed, because no microbes are present. Pasteurized milk will keep for a few days in the fridge before the small number of microbes left in it multiply and cause it to go sour. The low temperatures in the fridge slow down the rate at which microbes multiply. Once the container is opened all types of milk will go sour in two or three days at room temperature, because microbes from the air settle in the milk.

When microbes are being handled in laboratories it is best to assume that they are all harmful. People must take precautions to prevent microbes entering their bodies, such as not eating there.

Pickles Dried food

Canned food

Jams and preserves

Frozen food

Above: Some of the many ways of preserving food from decay by microbes. Food can be dried, pickled, canned, frozen or preserved in syrup.

Microbes in the laboratory

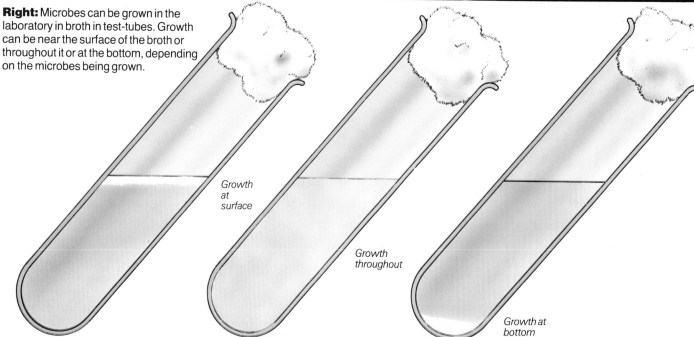

Right: Microbes can be grown in the laboratory in broth in test-tubes. Growth can be near the surface of the broth or throughout it or at the bottom, depending on the microbes being grown.

Growth at surface

Growth throughout

Growth at bottom

Under suitable conditions each cell of a microbe can divide to form two new cells once every 20 minutes. Although we can't see individual microbes without using a microscope, we can see large populations of them growing together as colonies. Colonies are groups of microbes, all of which have been produced from one original cell which has divided many times. Colonies appear after 1-2 days' growth.

In order to reproduce, microbes need a food supply, water and warmth. To grow microbes in the laboratory it is necessary to make sure that these conditions exist.

Food and containers

All equipment, including food and containers, must be sterilized before microbes are grown in the laboratory. Sterilization kills all microbes so that everything is absolutely clean and pure at the start. One of the ways to sterilize equipment is to heat it in a pressure-cooker for about half an hour. Sometimes a large 'pressure-cooker' called an autoclave is used. Apart from using heat to sterilize equipment, radiation and chemical disinfectants can also be used.

Microbes can be grown in bottles, flasks or dishes. The food can be liquid or solid. One very common way to grow microbes is to use a sterile shallow dish (a petri dish) containing agar. Agar is a

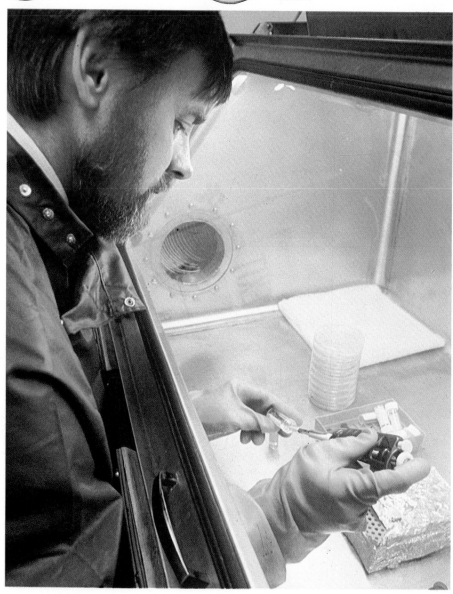

Right: Dangerous microbes must be used with great care. Here, a virus culture is being handled inside a sealed cabinet.

14

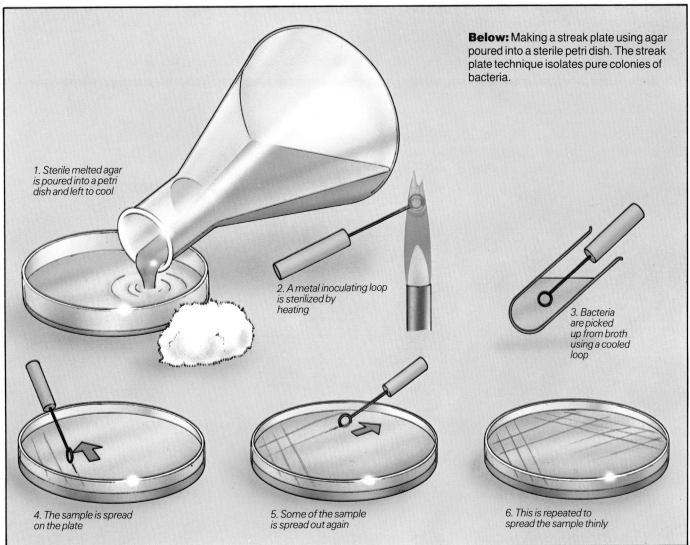

Below: Making a streak plate using agar poured into a sterile petri dish. The streak plate technique isolates pure colonies of bacteria.

jelly containing food microbes need and is obtained from seaweed. It is solid at room temperature but melts when warmed. Agar plates (or growth plates) are prepared by melting and pouring sterile agar into a sterile petri dish. The agar is then allowed to set before use.

Liquid foods in which microbes grow are called broths. They are formed by adding chemicals to water to form a clear liquid. The first broths were made from meat soups prepared in much the same way as making a stew. When microbes grow in broth it becomes cloudy. The more cloudy the broth the more microbes are present.

Adding the microbes

The introduction of microbes into the food supply is called inoculation. One easy way to add microbes to agar in sterile petri dishes is to remove the lid for a while. Microbes from the air settle in the agar and grow. Even if you breathe into sterile agar when the lid of a petri dish is slightly lifted, many microbes will grow. Pressing clean fingertips lightly onto sterile agar can produce surprising results when you see that some colonies of bacteria do grow.

Warmth

Once microbes have been introduced into the food in the containers, they are placed in a warm place for 1-2 days. This process is called incubation. An incubator or oven can be used to keep a constant temperature. During incubation the cells grow and divide giving rise to colonies on the agar. If only one type of microbe is present, all of the colonies will be identical. This is called a pure culture. It is much more likely that many different types of microbe will be growing so that the colonies look different. This is called a mixed culture. An inoculating loop can be used to pick up a sample of one colony and from this scientists can produce a pure culture using the streak plate technique.

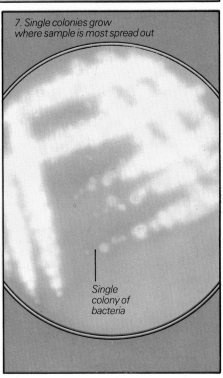

7. Single colonies grow where sample is most spread out

Single colony of bacteria

Growing microbes in industry

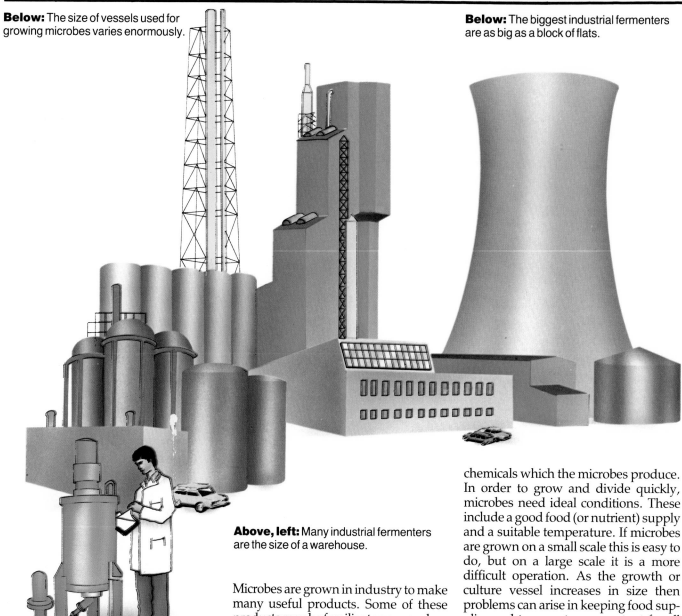

Microbes are grown in industry to make many useful products. Some of these products may be familiar to you, such as drugs and vitamins, but others are more unusual. For example, some microbes can produce a thick gum (Xanthan gum) which is used both in salad cream and in drilling muds in the oil industry. The bodies of other microbes can be dried to produce animal feed. And, of course, yeast extract comes from microbes.

These are just some of the many microbial products which are made on a large scale in industry.

Growing large numbers of microbes

Industrialists want to make money and therefore they want to grow large numbers of microbes in the shortest time possible in order to convert a cheap raw material into a saleable end product. These end products may be either the bodies of the microbes themselves or chemicals which the microbes produce. In order to grow and divide quickly, microbes need ideal conditions. These include a good food (or nutrient) supply and a suitable temperature. If microbes are grown on a small scale this is easy to do, but on a large scale it is a more difficult operation. As the growth or culture vessel increases in size then problems can arise in keeping food supplies and temperatures constant for all the microbes present.

Fermenters are growth vessels used in many industrial processes. A fermenter is a vessel in which microbes grow. The glass container used in home wine making is a fermenter. Industrial fermenters, however, are often very large and may be the size of a tall block of flats. It then becomes difficult to keep conditions constant. Another problem is that all the fermenter must be sterile otherwise undesirable microbes may grow and ruin the product.

The exact nutrients used in industry will depend upon the microbe involved and the product that is required. In the microbial production of vinegar, alcohol is used as a nutrient for vinegar-making bacteria. These bacteria convert the alcohol into vinegar.

A constant, suitable temperature is as

important as the nutrient supply. The exact temperature again depends upon the microbe used, but many that are used in the laboratory and in industry grow well between 20-40°C.

Growth vessels

These can be of various sizes, shapes and degrees of complexity. Growth of microbes in the vessels can be carried out in two possible ways. Some vessels use 'support-growth' systems. In this case the microbes grow as a layer or film on a surface which is in contact with the nutrients. An example of this is a dish or tray that contains a layer of nutrient. The microbes are grown on the surface of this. This method is used in the production of citric acid to be added to soft drinks. The technique was originally used in making penicillin. It is similar to growing microbes on a petri dish containing agar in the laboratory.

Other vessels use 'suspended-growth' systems. Here the microbes are scattered throughout (suspended in) the liquid medium. This type of vessel, or fermenter, has been used in the brewing industry for many years. The system is similar to growing microbes in a tube containing liquid broth in the school laboratory.

Once the growth vessel is in use, it may be run as a batch system or a continuous system. In a batch operation, the vessel is filled with the correct nutrients and the microbes, and suitable conditions are maintained to encourage microbial growth. After a time the vessel is emptied and cleaned. The product is purified and the whole process is repeated to make more product.

In the continuous operation, the vessel is filled with the correct nutrients and microbes and suitable conditions are maintained for microbial growth. However, fresh nutrients continuously enter the vessel while the end product and waste materials are continuously removed. The quantity of fresh nutrients continuously added is similar to the quantity of products which is continuously removed.

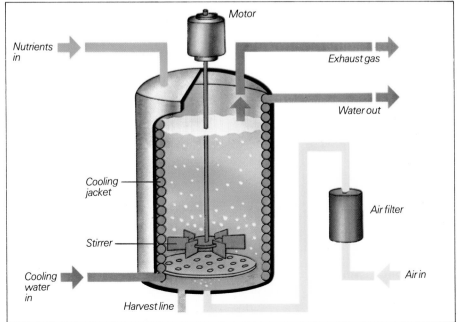

Left: A cross-section of an industrial fermenter showing the main parts which all fermenters have.

Familiar food from microbes

Above: Making Emmental cheese. The milk is heated to 33°C and then starter is added.

Above: Thick curd has now formed and it is cut into small pieces.

Above: The curd is strained in cheesecloth and the whey drains away.

For thousands of years microbes have been used to make different kinds of food and drink. It seems that it was purely by accident that people discovered that microbes were involved. It is thought that yoghurt was first produced when someone accidentally left milk too long before using it. The milk had thickened, and even though its flavour was different it was possible to eat it. Not for many years did people realize that microbes growing in the milk caused it to change to yoghurt.

The three main industries which use microbes to make foods and drinks nowadays are the dairy, baking and brewing industries.

The dairy industry
The role of microbes in the dairy industry starts on the farm where the cow is like a factory converting grass into milk.

Microbes in the cow's rumen help this process by their action in digesting the grass.

Once the milk has been produced, different types of microbes can be used to produce different types of food. For example, yoghurt is produced by the addition of lactic acid bacteria to warm milk which has been previously sterilized. These bacteria produce acid from part of the milk as they feed on it and the acid causes the milk to curdle and thicken, also giving the yoghurt its taste.

To make cheese, pasteurized milk is pumped into large vats. Meanwhile, 'starter' has been prepared in special tanks ready for addition to the milk. The starter is the basis of the whole cheese-making process and is a culture, in milk, of special bacteria grown under carefully controlled conditions. As in yoghurt manufacture, the bacteria make acid.

Different bacteria are used to produce different cheeses; each type gives the cheese its particular flavour and texture. The acid also preserves the cheese during storage.

Once the vats are filled with milk, rennet is added to make the milk thicken. Traditionally, rennet was obtained from the stomachs of calves, but may now be produced from microbes. The lumps formed by the action of the rennet are called curd and the liquid is called whey. The curd is drained and left to mature into the final cheese. The liquid whey is dried to form a powder which is used in cooked foods, animal feeds and the baking trade.

The baking industry
One of the main products of the baking industry is bread and the microbes used are yeasts. A dough is formed by knead-

Below: Barley, for beer-making. It is mixed with warm water to produce an extract called wort.

Below: The wort is boiled with hops in a brew kettle. Hops add flavour to the wort.

Below: Trays of drying yeast. Yeast, which ferments the wort, is the other ingredient in beer.

Above: The huge bag of wet curd is left to drain further.

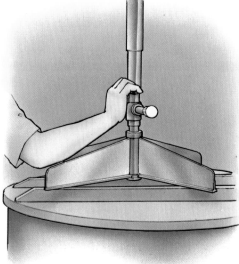

Above: The curd is pressed into a mould. The pressure gets rid of more whey.

Above: The compressed curd now looks like cheese. Salt is rubbed into it to help form the rind.

Left: Different kinds of bread can be made with different ingredients but these nearly always include yeast. Unleavened bread, made without yeast, can be seen in the bottom left corner.

Below: Yeast is added to the wort in a fermentation vessel. The froth is caused by bubbles of carbon dioxide.

ing together a mixture of flour, salt, water and yeast. Then the dough is left in a warm place, during which time it rises. The dough rises because the yeast cells ferment (respire without oxygen) and produce a gas called carbon dioxide. Bubbles of the gas trapped in the dough make it fluffy and light. The dough is then cut to shape and baked in an oven.

The brewing industry
In the brewing industry, many alcoholic drinks such as cider, wine and beer are made. Cider is made from apples, wine from grapes, and beer is made from malted barley. Hops are added to give

Below: After filtration and pasteurization, the beer is ready to be put into bottles or barrels.

beer its bitter flavour. In each case alcohol is produced when microbes, usually yeasts, convert the sugar present in the fruit, or vegetables, into alcohol during the process of fermentation. As well as alcohol, the gas carbon dioxide is also produced during fermentation. If trapped, this gas makes the drinks fizzy, like champagne, for example.

Different alcoholic drinks have such different tastes because of the variety of ingredients used to make them and because of differences in the way they are made. But using different yeasts can also affect the flavour, particularly in wine-making.

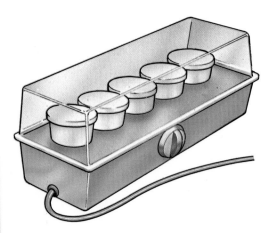

Above: Yoghurt can easily be made using heated milk with some yoghurt added as 'starter'. This home yoghurt-maker keeps the temperature constant.

New foods from microbes

At present the human population of the world is about four billion and increasing rapidly. By the year 2000 it is estimated that more than six billion people will be alive. This means there is an ever-increasing demand for food. An increase in food production by conventional methods, such as farming, may not, on its own, be enough to solve the food shortage problem. It will be necessary to find new sources of food.

Microbes can be used to make some kinds of new foods for both animals and humans. They may help to overcome food shortage in some parts of the world. But although microbes are a cheap source of food and can be used to make large quantities of it, the cost of the technology involved in producing such food is very high.

Single-cell protein production

One of the main types of food which is in short supply is protein. It is necessary for healthy growth and repair of body tissues. Foods rich in proteins, such as

meat, are expensive. Meat is particularly expensive because the animals from which the meat is produced are fed on plants which in turn have been specially produced.

The cells of certain bacteria are rich in protein, and so they are used in single cell protein (SCP) production. SCP can be produced from bacteria which are grown in bulk, then dried and made into powder or pellets to be used as animal feed.

In the SCP process, a few litres of bacterial culture are placed in a large fermenter which has first been sterilized with steam. The fermenter is then filled with sterilized water, methanol, ammonia and other nutrients. The methanol is an alcohol produced from natural gas. (In some kinds of SCP production, chemicals other than methanol may be used, such as products from refining oil.)

The bacteria are then allowed to grow in the methanol and reproduce so that within two days, 60 tonnes of bacterial

cells are formed. Most of these cells are removed and dried to make SCP. There is a continuous replacement of fresh nutrients into the fermenter, so that the process could work non-stop for about six months. In this time vast quantities of protein food could be made.

This process may be very useful because the processing plant takes up a relatively small area of land compared to the vast areas of fields used for conventional methods of growing food. The process also works well no matter what the weather is like outside. It is therefore a possible method of producing food on land which would not normally be used for food production.

At present SCP is fed to animals such as calves or chickens. The high quality of the product suggests that it may be suitable for human food. But the SCP will have to be processed further so that it is not harmful to humans and this will increase the cost of the product.

Food from algae

Algae are simple plants that grow in water. Many algae are rich in proteins, vitamins and minerals, all of which are needed by animals to survive. The alga *Spirulina* was collected from lakes and prepared as food many hundreds of years ago by Aztec Indians. After drying in the Sun, it has a mild taste. It can contain up to 70% protein and therefore provides much more protein than many cultivated vegetables, even protein-rich ones such as peas or beans.

If cattle are farmed to produce beef protein they yield 100 kilograms of protein per hectare of grazing land, per year. If *Spirulina* were grown to produce protein it would yield up to 50,000 kilograms of protein per hectare of land used, per year. In some hot countries like Israel, algae are already farmed in large ponds.

All that algae need to make their own food is sunlight and water. Green plants, such as algae, carry out the process of photosynthesis in the light and convert carbon dioxide from the air plus water into foods such as protein. In many desert areas it is very difficult to grow crops, but if large holes are lined with polythene to make ponds and then filled with water and algae, large quanti-

Left: Using microbes for food is not a new idea. Hundreds of years ago, the Aztec Indians strained the alga *Spirulina* from lakes to dry and eat.

ties of food can be made, especially if a 'greenhouse' is made over the pond by enclosing it with a transparent polythene tunnel. Some algae will even grow well in salt water. The algae grow rapidly and after harvesting, the cells can be dried to make a protein-rich food.

Steaks from fungi

We eat mushrooms, which are fungi. Very soon we may be eating other fungi which are very rich in protein. One type of fungus can be grown on waste starches (from processing potatoes for example) inside large fermenters. The fungi are extracted and can be used to make artificial meat when flavourings are added. The fungus is made into artificial meat because the strands of fungus are similar to strands of meat. This gives the fungus a meaty texture and makes it more attractive to us.

If you are not already doing so now, you may soon be eating the dried bodies of bacteria, algae or fungi, instead of (or as well as) conventional foods, such as meat, vegetables or cheese.

Right: Nowadays, *Spirulina* is cultivated in artificial ponds in Israel. The alga has a high protein content.

Below: The process of single cell protein production from methane.

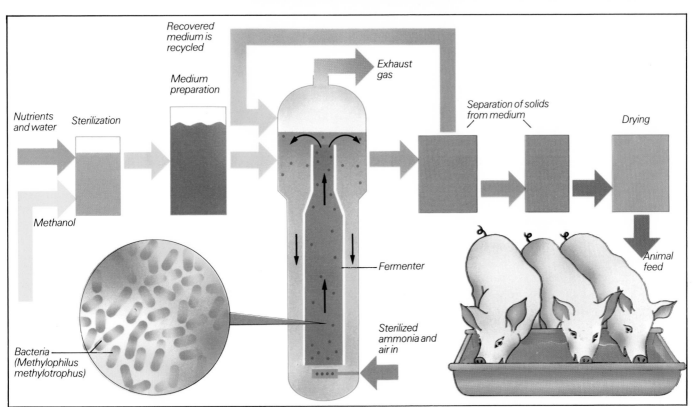

Recovered medium is recycled

Medium preparation

Exhaust gas

Nutrients and water

Sterilization

Separation of solids from medium

Drying

Methanol

Fermenter

Animal feed

Bacteria (Methylophilus methylotrophus)

Sterilized ammonia and air in

Microbes and enzymes

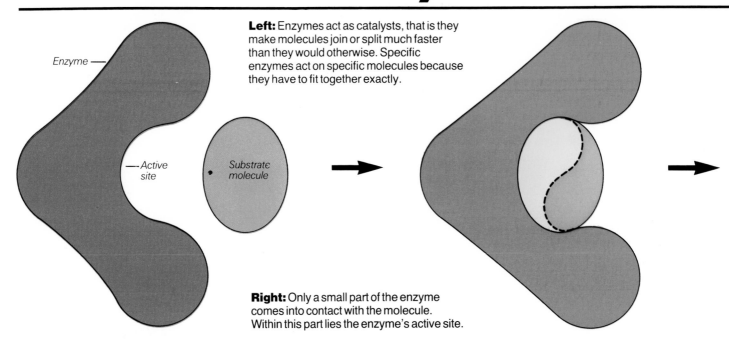

Left: Enzymes act as catalysts, that is they make molecules join or split much faster than they would otherwise. Specific enzymes act on specific molecules because they have to fit together exactly.

Enzyme

Active site

Substrate molecule

Right: Only a small part of the enzyme comes into contact with the molecule. Within this part lies the enzyme's active site.

Many microbes can carry out the process of fermentation and in doing so they convert sugars into alcohol. This forms the basis of the brewing industry. But do the microbes themselves need to be present for the conversion process to take place? In 1897 two German scientists were preparing yeast extracts and to preserve the juice they obtained, they added sugar to it. It fermented rapidly. No microbes were present, so the juice alone must have been responsible for the fermentation which occurred.

What these scientists had discovered was enzyme activity. Since then it has been shown that not only fermentation, but all other acitivities in all living cells of all living things, is controlled by these special chemicals called enzymes.

What are enzymes?

Enzymes are complex chemicals which help living things to carry out chemical reactions inside their bodies. These re-actions are necessary in growing, breathing and all the other activities of life. Enzymes are catalysts, that is they speed up chemical reactions inside living cells. But the enzymes themselves are needed in only very small quantities and are not used up at the end of the reaction. Thus they can be re-used.

You may well have heard of enzymes involved in digestion. There is, for example, an enzyme in your saliva which breaks down starch, from such food as bread or potatoes, into sugars which your body can more easily use for energy. Enzymes are important in many other processes as well as digestion.

Even at body temperature, enzymes enable reactions to occur quickly. Catalysts used in the chemical industry work well only at a very high temperature. People have found it very difficult or even impossible to copy the way in which enzymes work. This fact has encouraged scientists to obtain enzymes from the living things that produce them. Microbial enzymes are now used in many industries to make a variety of useful products.

Uses of enzymes

Even though you may not have realized it, enzymes obtained from microbes have probably already found their way

Left: Inside a factory making soft-centred chocolates. An enzyme called invertase is mixed with the sugary filling and this acts on the filling, inside the chocolate coating, making it go soft.

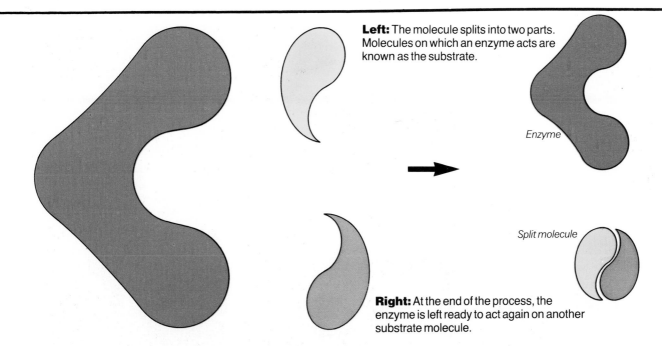

Left: The molecule splits into two parts. Molecules on which an enzyme acts are known as the substrate.

Enzyme

Split molecule

Right: At the end of the process, the enzyme is left ready to act again on another substrate molecule.

into your home. When the first biological washing powders were sold in the 1960s they proved a great success. The washing powder in your home is almost certainly biological. 'Biological' in this sense means that the washing powder contains enzymes which enable it to get rid of dirt stains even at low temperatures. These enzymes include proteases which break down proteins and so they get rid of stains such as egg or blood. The problem is that people with sensitive skins may get a rash because they react to the traces of enzymes left on the clothes.

Have you ever used barbecue sauce? This also contains proteases which help to make the meat more tender. Other enzymes, such as pectolase, are used in home wine-making kits.

So enzymes do have uses in the home, but their main use is in industry. Traditional processes such as brewing, baking and cheese-making can now be carried out by means of extracted enzymes. Such enzymes are used in the leather and textile industries for softening leather and removing chemicals, such as starch, from fabrics. The future of the enzyme industry looks bright as more types of microbes are 'persuaded' to produce new enzymes.

Below: A range of washing powders on sale in a supermarket. Most of them contain enzymes.

Microbes, chemicals and fuels

Above: An operational system using enzymes in industry. The enzymes inside are fixed on layers of material such as charcoal and this gives a larger yield of product at less cost.

Below: A fuel pump in Brazil serving alcohol for use in vehicles.

Coal, oil and natural gas are commonly used in industry and in our homes as fuels. All three fuels were made millions of years ago when the dead remains of plants and animals were acted upon by microbes and by pressure from the rock layers deposited above.

It has been predicted, however, that our reserves of coal, oil and gas will be exhausted early next century if we continue to use them at the present rate. It is essential, therefore, that alternative sources of fuel be found. Several alternatives are available, one being to produce fuels on a large scale using microbes. Two such fuels are alcohol and methane. Microbially-produced fuels are a 'renewable resource' because once they have been used up, more fuel can be made whereas coal, oil and natural gas cannot be replaced once they have been used.

Alcohol production

Microbes are capable of mass-producing alcohol for many purposes, other than as drinks. Alcohol acts as a solvent for a wide range of products, including paints, dyes and lacquers. (A solvent is a chemical in which other chemicals dissolve.) Some alcohol is used as a starting material in the microbial production of single cell protein, but alcohol can also be used as a fuel. It can be used as a substitute for certain oil products such as petrol.

It has already been mentioned that the process of alcohol production by microbes is called fermentation. For fermentation to occur the microbes must have a supply of sugar or starch. Usually the source of sugar is the sugar cane plant, but other crops such as sugar beet may also be used. Once made the alcohol must be extracted and purified before it is ready for use.

Alcohol, as a fuel, is particularly attractive to countries which may be unable to afford to import oil and have no oil source of their own, but have large areas of land to grow a sugar source. In Brazil, for example, a government scheme was set up in 1975 to produce alcohol by sugar cane fermentation. By

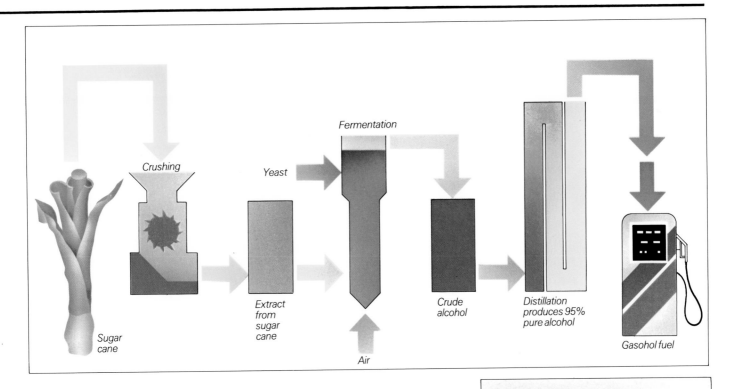

Sugar cane

Crushing

Yeast

Fermentation

Extract from sugar cane

Air

Crude alcohol

Distillation produces 95% pure alcohol

Gasohol fuel

1981 the Brazilians had one car in six running on an alcohol/petrol mixture known as gasohol.

Methane production

If alcohol is an alternative liquid fuel to petrol then methane is an equivalent alternative to natural gas. In fact, natural gas contains a lot of methane. If gas from oil fields is all used up what are the alternative sources? One of the products from humans and animals which is in plentiful supply is faeces or manure. In recent years cattle, pig and chicken production has increased rapidly. Sewage production from humans also increases as the world population increases. Many microbes are able to produce methane as a by-product of their feeding processes when they live on waste such as sewage or manure.

In developing countries small-scale waste processors are plentiful. Sewage and manure are collected in tanks, where the microbes present release methane gas over a period of time. This can be used for cooking and heating purposes. The residue can be treated to make fertilizer for use on the land.

On a large scale, in industrial areas, methane fermenters are used in sewage works. In many such works this is already being done and the methane produced is used as a fuel, usually for processes involved in sewage treatment. Methane can even be used instead of petrol to run tractors or cars.

Above: Producing fuel from sugar cane. An extract from crushed sugar cane is fermented and then distilled to produce ethanol (alcohol).

Below: A 'biogas' generator of the type used in India. Microbes act on animal waste, such as cattle manure, to produce methane gas.

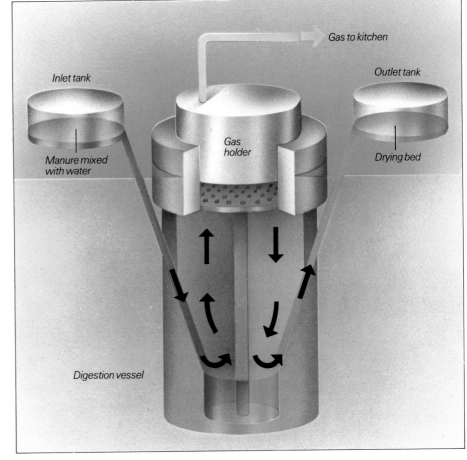

Inlet tank

Manure mixed with water

Gas to kitchen

Gas holder

Outlet tank

Drying bed

Digestion vessel

Waste treatment

Below: In nineteenth century London, many children died from diseases which spread rapidly because of sewage flowing through the streets. This cartoon from that period shows the figure of Death rising from the open sewer where children play.

The problems of removal of waste have existed since humans started to live together in villages and towns. Early in human history, waste or sewage would often simply be thrown into streets where people and animals would walk. It is not surprising that diseases such as cholera and typhoid were then so common, killing thousands of people each year.

This risk to health was recognized as early as Roman times, when a system of large sewers was built in Rome to remove human waste safely. Although today we may take waste treatment and water purification for granted, it is certain that without techniques of sewage removal and treatment such diseases as typhoid and cholera would be common even in countries like Britain which have a cool climate. Until fairly recently it was common practice throughout the world for untreated sewage to be poured into rivers or seas. For reasons of pollution control and hygiene, countries which can afford to build sewage treatment plants now treat their sewage to make it safe before it enters rivers or seas. Many developing countries still cannot afford to build systems of sewers everywhere and so they still have outbreaks of cholera and typhoid. Such epidemics may affect thousands of people.

Above: The pollution due to untreated waste flowing into the sea can be seen clearly here.

Below: Septic tanks are still commonly used in many areas for treating sewage. The sediment in the two parts of the tank has to be cleaned out occasionally.

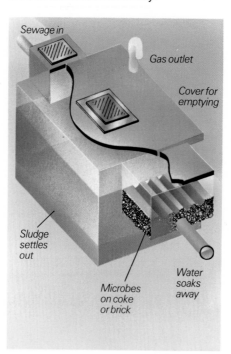

Sewage in

Gas outlet

Cover for emptying

Sludge settles out

Microbes on coke or brick

Water soaks away

Small-scale sewage treatment

One of the oldest devices for treating sewage is the septic tank. In many areas of the world it is still used where there are just a few isolated houses. The septic tank consists of a large sealed tank which is usually buried in the ground.

Two pipes enter the tank. One pipe allows the sewage to enter, the other allows the treated water to flow out. As the sewage enters the tank, any solid material suspended in it settles, because of the effect of gravity, to the bottom of the tank. Populations of naturally occurring microbes begin to digest the settled solids, producing methane gas as a by-product. As the water passes across the tank more and more solid matter settles until eventually the cleared water can be poured into a nearby river or may just escape into the soil.

Large-scale sewage treatment

When dealing with sewage produced by a big town or city, larger scale methods of treatment must be employed to reduce the risks of infection. Two of the main methods of treatment used nowadays are the biological filtration process and the activated sludge process.

In the biological filtration process the sewage is first filtered to remove solids by passing it through a series of metal screens. Next the filtered sewage is allowed to settle to remove any remaining solids that may have escaped filtration. The remaining fluid trickles through a biological filter. This may be made of soil, clinker or stones, but in each case a surface film of microbes develops on the particles. These microbes digest waste. The extracted solids may be allowed to dry or may be further digested by microbes and can be used as fertilizer. The treated water, which by now is fairly pure, is released into the river or sea.

If this water is to be made fit for humans to drink, it must be passed through a water purification plant. Here the water is first stored in reservoirs. Exposure of the water to air and sunlight helps kill off some of the harmful microbes. The water is then filtered slowly through layers of sand and gravel. Microbes grow as a coat on the sand and gravel particles and bring about natural purification of the water. As a safeguard, small quantities of chlorine are added to the water. The chlorine kills any remaining harmful microbes. Not too much chlorine is added, however, or our drinking water might taste like water in a swimming pool! The water is tested for purity before distribution.

A lot of purified water from sewage works goes back into drinking water reservoirs. It has been estimated that drinking water in London has already passed through seven people before it reaches London!

In the activated sludge process, after the sewage has been allowed to settle in one tank, the liquid is pumped into a second tank and has air or oxygen forced through it. This causes the solids and the microbes in the sewage to collect together and to form floating mats. These mats attract other suspended matter which collects to be digested by the microbes that already exist there. The waste is then filtered and liquids pass into rivers or the sea, while solids can be used as fertilizer. This method has the advantages that it occupies a smaller area and works faster than the biological filtration method.

Sewage plants deal with human waste products in an efficient and hygienic way. They may also be the source of useful by-products. It has already been mentioned that methane can be used as a fuel. Also the dried, treated, solid matter can be used as an inexpensive and rich source of nutrients as a fertilizer in agriculture.

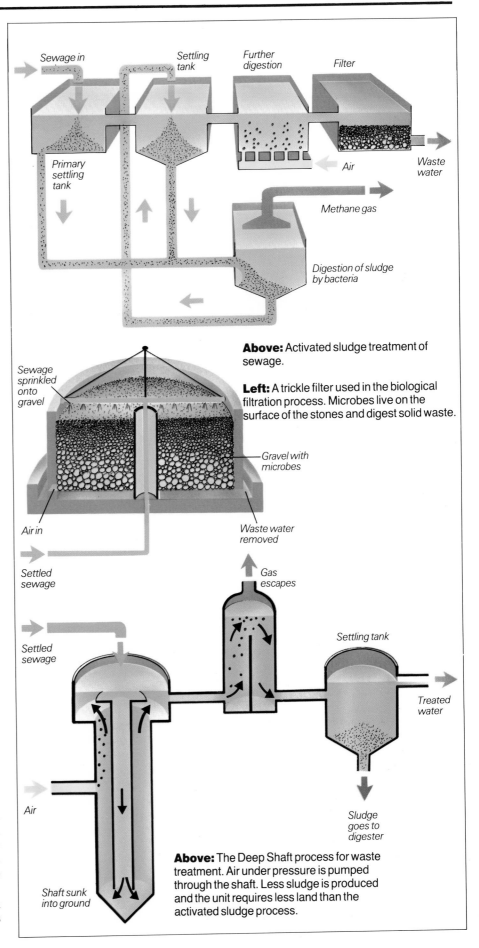

Above: Activated sludge treatment of sewage.

Left: A trickle filter used in the biological filtration process. Microbes live on the surface of the stones and digest solid waste.

Above: The Deep Shaft process for waste treatment. Air under pressure is pumped through the shaft. Less sludge is produced and the unit requires less land than the activated sludge process.

Microbes, soil and agriculture

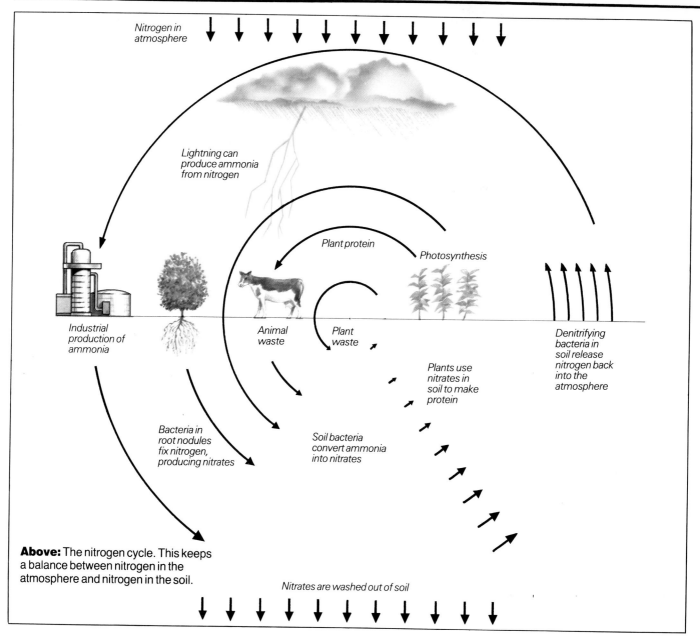

Nitrogen in atmosphere

Lightning can produce ammonia from nitrogen

Plant protein

Photosynthesis

Industrial production of ammonia

Animal waste

Plant waste

Denitrifying bacteria in soil release nitrogen back into the atmosphere

Plants use nitrates in soil to make protein

Bacteria in root nodules fix nitrogen, producing nitrates

Soil bacteria convert ammonia into nitrates

Above: The nitrogen cycle. This keeps a balance between nitrogen in the atmosphere and nitrogen in the soil.

Nitrates are washed out of soil

Agriculture relies heavily on microbes, either to keep the soil fertile or produce animal feed or help fight against pests.

Microbes in the soil
One cubic centimetre of soil can contain six to ten million bacteria and one to two kilometres of fungal strands. These fungi and bacteria together can feed upon all naturally occurring compounds and most artificially-made ones as well. In doing so they decompose, or decay, the wastes and dead remains of plants and animals in the soil. Nutrients which were present in the bodies of these organisms are set free or re-cycled by microbes to be used again. If this did not occur then the soil would soon become infertile, with no plant growth.

Microbes also help soil fertility by making nitrogen available to growing plants. Nitrogen is an essential component of proteins, which plants and animals need to build new cells. There is plenty of nitrogen in the air, but plants and animals cannot use it directly from the air. Instead, plants obtain their nitrogen in the form of nitrates, which they absorb from the soil. Animals obtain their nitrogen by eating plants. If all of the nitrates from the soil were used up then plant growth would stop and animals would die because they would have no food. A balance of nitrates is kept in the soil by the action of certain microbes, which produce nitrates by decomposition of dead plants and animals.

Some bacteria can convert nitrogen from the air directly into nitrates. Some of these nitrogen-fixing bacteria live in the soil and some live in the swellings or nodules on the roots of legumes. Legumes are plants such as peas, beans and clover. They use the nitrate produced by the bacteria so they have in-built 'fertilizers' in the form of microbes. Other plants need the addition of fertilizers for healthy growth. These fertilizers can be either artificial or natural fertilizers such as compost or manure – plant and animal waste which microbes decompose.

Much work is being carried out at present on developing agricultural crops (such as cereals and rice) which have root nodules containing nitrogen-fixing bacteria as do legumes. If this is successful then healthy crops could be grown without the use of expensive artificial fertilizers.

Above: Nodules on the root of a bean plant. These nodules contain bacteria which fix nitrogen from the air and so provide the plant with nitrates.

Below: Chemical insecticides sprayed on crops can have harmful effects as they pass through the food chain because they may accumulate in body tissues.

Above: Swarms of thousands of locusts can completely destroy crops as they move from area to area to feed. Protection of crops is necessary.

Microbes and silage

Silage is made from crops and is used as an animal feed, especially during winter months. The process involves the controlled fermentation for 3-4 weeks, by bacteria, of the sugar present in green crops such as grass or maize to produce acids and proteins. To make silage the green crop is packed and compressed to remove air. Silage is more nutritional and more easily digested than other winter foods such as hay.

Spraying insecticide

Microbes and insecticides

Crops can be severely damaged by insects so that food production is reduced. A number of chemical insecticides have been used, but these often upset the balance of nature and are poisonous to animals and humans. It was recently discovered that certain bacteria could naturally produce insecticides. One of these kills caterpillars which cause damage to fruit trees. Such insecticides are only harmful to the insects.

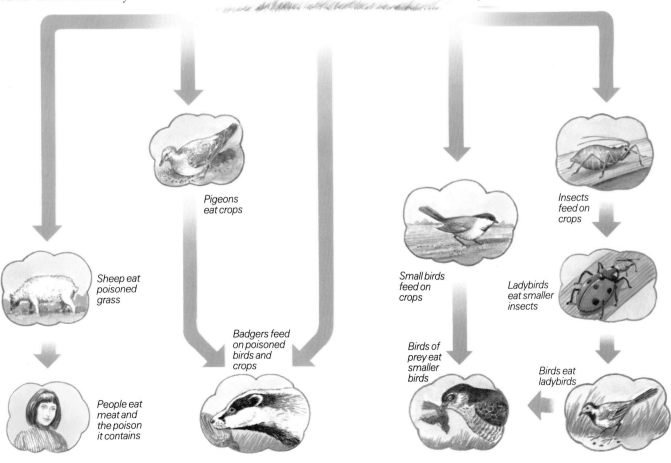

Pigeons eat crops

Sheep eat poisoned grass

Badgers feed on poisoned birds and crops

People eat meat and the poison it contains

Small birds feed on crops

Insects feed on crops

Ladybirds eat smaller insects

Birds of prey eat smaller birds

Birds eat ladybirds

Plant diseases

If you keep fruit too long before eating it, it becomes discoloured and starts to rot. If you over-water young seedlings they often rot at the base, and fall over and die. Both of these are examples of fairly common plant diseases caused by microbes. The seedlings described have caught 'damping-off disease' which is caused by a fungus. But how can this disease be prevented, since young plants need water? One way is to add a chemical called a fungicide to the water. This kills the fungi and allows the plant to grow.

Ever since people began to cultivate crops, plant diseases have been a problem. In modern farming systems large areas of land may be covered by one kind of crop only. In this case great care must be taken to prevent plant diseases from occurring, otherwise the entire crop could be killed.

The importance of plant diseases

Because people depend on plants for a large proportion of the food that they eat, the destruction of crops due to plant diseases can be very serious indeed. It may cause famines which result in the deaths of many people.

Such a famine happened in Ireland in the 1840s. At that time the main food of the Irish poor was potatoes. A fungus called potato blight attacked the potato crops causing the plants to wilt and die. The fungus also attacked the potato tubers underground and caused them to rot. The disease spread rapidly throughout the entire country. This meant that there was little food available and one million people died. Two million people emigrated to avoid the famine.

During the 1950s, in the USA alone, an estimated three million dollars' worth of agricultural produce was lost due to plant diseases. It is certain that losses in the tropics are much higher than this. In modern developed countries such losses may have little direct effect on the population as these countries can afford to import extra food. In less wealthy countries, any loss in crop production has an immediate effect on the population and can lead to famines and the death of thousands of people. These people have no money available to import food from other countries.

Left: Plant diseases can destroy much-needed food. These apples are rotting on the tree because of microbial attack.

Below: People attacking a potato store during the Irish potato famine. Potato blight had made their staple food so scarce people would fight for it.

From this you can see that it is important for scientists to be able to tell which organism causes a particular disease and to attempt to find ways of preventing such diseases from occurring.

Common plant diseases

Gardeners are familiar with common plant diseases causing rot in carrots and cabbage, for example, or mildew on roses. These diseases can usually be prevented by using an appropriate chemical treatment. Dutch elm disease affects trees and is harder to get rid of. It is caused by a fungus and was first observed in Europe in 1918 and reached Britain in 1927. In the 1930s many elm trees were affected by this disease. It did not become an important problem again until the 1970s, when thousands of elm

Right: Plant diseases can still cause famine in poor countries. Here, people have to queue for scarce supplies of food.

Below: Spraying an apple crop by helicopter to prevent damage to the crop.

trees were damaged and died in Britain.

To infect the tree, the fungus must enter the living parts of the tree through a wound. These wounds are often made by a small beetle which burrows through the bark of the tree. The spores of the fungus are carried on the legs of

the beetle and are deposited in the wounds. Here the fungus germinates, grows and spreads throughout the tree to eventually cause its death. In many young elms death can occur within two weeks of being infected.

Unfortunately the fungus does not die with the tree. It continues to use the dead tree as a source of food. At about this time the beetle, which has been continually burrowing under the bark of the tree, lays eggs. These hatch and develop into young beetles. When these young beetles fly to another tree they take the fungal spores with them.

Preventing plant diseases

There are several methods of preventing plant diseases. Infected plants can be sprayed with chemicals. These kill the disease-causing microbe without harming the plant. Many plant diseases are treated with copper compounds which kill the microbes causing the damage. In severe outbreaks of plant diseases it may be necessary to destroy the entire crop to prevent further spread of the disease.

Nowadays, disease-resistant plants are being bred so that they do not catch the disease in the first place.

Animal diseases

Human and animal diseases have been a problem since life began. It was not until the nineteenth century, however, that the connection between microbes and diseases was demonstrated. Much of the important work in this area was carried out by two very famous micro-biologists, Louis Pasteur and Robert Koch. Since their time many discoveries have been made about human and animal diseases.

A small percentage of the many types of microbes have the ability to cause infectious disease. The microbes act as parasites when they live on or in the bodies of humans, animals or plants, which are the hosts. The parasites cause damage to the host. If the microbe is very active in causing damage (that is, viru-

lent) then disease occurs. If the host is able to restrict the growth of the microbe (that is, resistant) then the host remains healthy. A disease is a process not a thing. The outcome of the interaction between the host and the parasite leads to damage to the host.

Most young people can resist infection to pneumonia which is a disease most commonly caused by bacteria. (One type of pneumonia is caused by a virus.) However, old people, particular-

Left: Robert Koch at work in his laboratory.

Below: Chickenpox is a common childhood disease. It is caused by a virus.

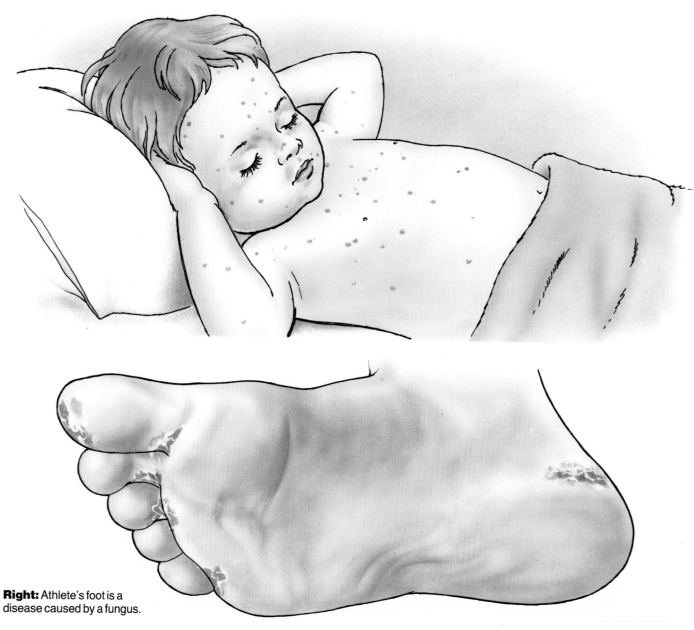

Right: Athlete's foot is a disease caused by a fungus.

Below: Cholera spreads easily when sewage contaminates supplies of drinking water.

Sewage

Contaminated water is drunk

ly ones who are so weak they have to stay in bed, may catch pneumonia because their resistance is low and they are less able to fight off the infection.

Before it can cause damage, any microbe must first enter the body of the host. It can do this through an opening such as the mouth or nose or through the skin if it is cut. Bacteria which cause pneumonia enter through the nose and in healthy people will not have any effect. If the disease occurs, it damages the lungs.

Human diseases
Bacteria which cause tetanus often exist in soil and dust and enter the skin through a wound. It is therefore advisable to have an injection against tetanus if you have accidentally wounded yourself, by, for example, standing on an old rusty nail. Microbes cause disease in the bodies of humans or animals by producing waste products called toxins. The tetanus toxin causes muscles to go into spasm and the disease kills because it stops people breathing.

Two common human illnesses are colds and 'flu. Both of these are caused by different types of viruses. The symptoms are fever, headache and a runny nose. The body is able to fight against the viruses causing these symptoms and recovery follows after a few days.

Until recently smallpox was an important human disease because it was particularly nasty and dangerous and resulted in the death of almost 40% of the people who caught the disease. The symptoms are a high fever, aching limbs and back and the development of large spots. These become filled with pus. If the person survives the smallpox attack, the spots dry and leave scars. But smallpox has now been eliminated throughout the world because people were vaccinated so that they did not catch the disease and so the virus could not live.

Cholera and typhoid are diseases caused by bacteria. These diseases are normally spread by drinking infected water and result in symptoms which include fever and diarrhoea. Athlete's foot is a fungal disease which was described earlier.

Diseases of other animals
Rabies is a fatal disease, caused by a virus, and occurs in dogs and other flesh-eating animals. It can also affect humans if they have been bitten by a rabid animal. In animals the symptoms of the disease are foaming of the mouth and aggressive behaviour. Humans who catch the disease (from a dog bite, usually) can be treated but this may not be successful and they suffer convulsions and paralysis before death results. Rabies is not present in Britain and so there are strict controls on bringing in animals from other countries. There are posters at the ports forbidding people to unlawfully bring in animals. Those animals which are allowed to enter undergo a long period of quarantine to make sure they don't have the disease.

Foot and mouth disease affects cattle and pigs. It can spread rapidly from farm to farm as it is caused by an air-borne virus. Infected animals lose weight and milk production in cows is reduced. Blisters and spots form on the tongue and mouth. These spots contain the virus. When the spots burst, millions of viruses are spread into the air and may be carried long distances by the wind. It is very difficult to control the spread of this disease and because it is expensive to vaccinate animals to stop them getting it, it is cheaper to stamp out the disease by slaughtering the whole herd of animals, even if they do not all show the disease symptoms.

Treatment and prevention
In extreme cases diseased animals, such

as those suffering from foot and mouth disease, are killed. Quarantine, already mentioned in connection with rabies, is a method of keeping a human or animal in isolation, in an attempt to prevent certain infectious diseases from spreading.

But animals, including humans, have an in-built defence system against disease. This system involves white blood cells and antibodies. If these mechanisms stop the disease-causing microbes from multiplying quickly then the body remains healthy. If the microbial growth is uncontrolled by the white blood cells and antibodies then disease results. Recovery may occur when the harmful microbes are brought under control by extra production of white blood cells and antibodies.

Vaccinations can be given against certain diseases as a preventative measure. Drugs, such as antibiotics, can be given to treat bacterial infections, once signs of the disease show.

Below: Myxomatosis is a fatal viral disease of rabbits. One symptom is swelling around the eyes. The disease has been used to control the size of rabbit populations, since rabbits can cause damage to crops when they eat them.

Vaccines

Above: Louis Pasteur carried out much research on microbes and established how vaccines prevent disease.

Left: Edward Jenner developed a vaccine against smallpox in the eighteenth century.

One of the ways to prevent disease of humans and animals from developing is vaccination. Pioneer work on vaccination was carried out in 1798 by Edward Jenner, who was an English country doctor. At that time smallpox was a very common disease in England and was responsible for many deaths. Jenner noticed that people who had suffered from cowpox, a similar, but less severe, disease, were able to resist later infection by smallpox.

Jenner took some of the material from a sore on the hands of a local milk maid who was suffering from cowpox. He then scratched this material into the skin on the arm of a completely healthy boy. The boy developed cowpox on his hands, but was otherwise healthy. Jenner then exposed the same boy to material from the skin of a smallpox sufferer. Fortunately the boy did not develop smallpox – he was immune to the disease. The test was repeated some months later but the boy still remained immune to smallpox. Jenner repeated these tests on a number of different people. The results were all the same. Exposure to cowpox produced immunity to smallpox.

Jenner was the first person to scientifically demonstrate by these experiments that the technique of vaccination could protect against a disease. Although Jenner's vaccination worked, he did not know why vaccination with cowpox should protect against smallpox. Louis Pasteur established how vaccines worked to prevent disease from developing. Once it was understood how vaccines work it was not long before they were being produced to protect against a number of different diseases such as diphtheria and tetanus.

How vaccines work

Vaccination is a technique which stimulates the body's own natural defence system before it catches a given disease. If the disease-causing microbes later enter the body they are destroyed before any harm can be done. In Britain, for example, nearly all young children are given a polio vaccination. This stimulates the defence mechanisms of the body so that the child is protected from developing polio later on in life.

Three types of vaccines are commonly used: firstly, weakened living microbes which cause the disease; secondly, dead microbes that would have caused the disease; and finally, poisonous substances produced by the microbes that cause the disease. No matter which type of vaccine is used, they all work in basically the same way.

The vaccine is first introduced into the

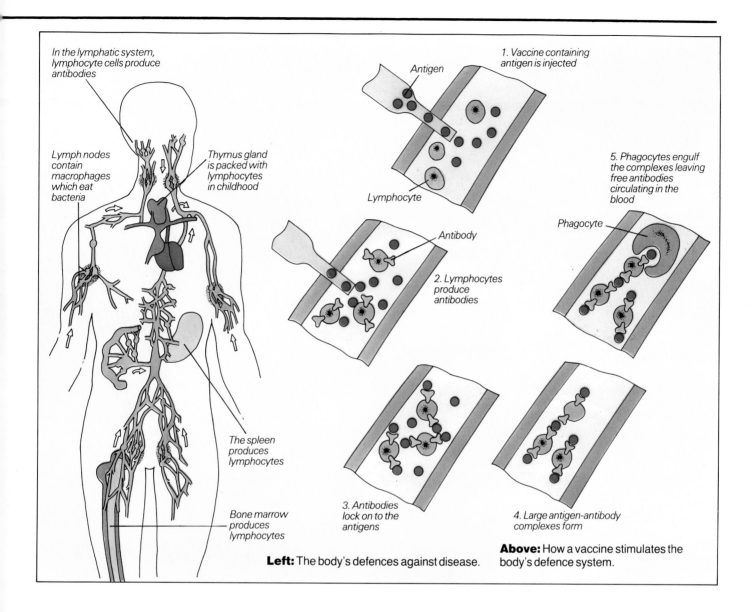

In the lymphatic system, lymphocyte cells produce antibodies

Lymph nodes contain macrophages which eat bacteria

Thymus gland is packed with lymphocytes in childhood

The spleen produces lymphocytes

Bone marrow produces lymphocytes

Antigen

1. Vaccine containing antigen is injected

Lymphocyte

Antibody

2. Lymphocytes produce antibodies

3. Antibodies lock on to the antigens

5. Phagocytes engulf the complexes leaving free antibodies circulating in the blood

Phagocyte

4. Large antigen-antibody complexes form

Left: The body's defences against disease.

Above: How a vaccine stimulates the body's defence system.

bloodstream, usually by injection. The presence of the vaccine material causes the body's own defence mechanisms to release substances called antibodies. These are special proteins produced by certain white blood cells.

Some protein parts of microbial cells may act as antigens. These are part of the disease-causing system. Antibodies encounter the invading material (antigens) and join with it. This acts as a signal to other white blood cells, called phagocytes, to eat such antibody-antigen complexes. The effect of the harmful microbe is removed and therefore disease is prevented.

Antibodies are specific. They only join with certain antigens, so that one type of antibody will prevent one particular disease. Even after the invading material has been got rid of, some of the antibodies produced in response to that invader remain in the bloodstream. If the same type of invading microbe later attempts to enter the body of the vaccinated person, the microbe is immediately destroyed due to the presence of the antibodies.

When the body is protected from a disease we say it is immune to it. Vaccination results in artificial immunity. Natural immunity occurs when a person has a mild attack of a disease so that the body's defence system is stimulated and gives protection against further attacks.

Vaccines today

Nowadays there are vaccines to protect us against most diseases. Vaccination against polio is unusual because it is given through the mouth, on a sugar lump. As well as the polio vaccine most young children receive a single injection of a triple vaccine. This protects against diphtheria, tetanus and whooping cough. Vaccines against smallpox, measles, German measles and tuberculosis are also commonly used and more are being developed.

Not all children are automatically given a course of vaccinations that includes all of the six vaccines mentioned. Some children may be at risk to possible harm if they receive a given type of vaccine. For example, the whooping cough vaccine may result in severe brain damage in some children. Their bodies' defence systems cannot cope even with the weakened form of the disease in a vaccine and damage is caused.

But it is fair to say that vaccines have played an extremely important part in reducing deaths from a number of harmful diseases. In fact, vaccines have resulted in the complete eradication of some diseases, such as smallpox.

Antibiotics

Once a disease has become established it is necessary to treat it so that the disease is destroyed and any harmful effects are kept to a minimum. Today diseases are treated by using various chemicals that cause harm to the invading microbes without – most importantly – harming the patient. These chemicals may be given as injections or as medicines or tablets.

Various microbes produce naturally occurring chemicals that can be used to treat diseases. The fungi are a particularly important group in this respect. The substances they produce which can be used to cure diseases are called antibiotics. These stop the growth of other microbes or even destroy them. Today many different kinds of antibiotics are being produced in industry to help in the fight against disease.

History of antibiotics
Penicillin was the first antibiotic to be discovered. Its discovery occurred as the result of a chance observation by Alexander Fleming in 1928. Fleming was growing colonies of bacteria on agar plates in his laboratory. He left the plates on his desk while he went away on holiday. When he returned he examined the plates and noticed that a colony of mould was growing on one side of the plate. The mould must have

settled from the air and grown while Fleming was away. Near the mould the bacterial growth was poor but further away from the mould the colonies of bacteria were larger. Fleming correctly deduced that the mould was in some way preventing the growth of the bacteria.

The mould which stopped bacteria growing in Fleming's laboratory was a

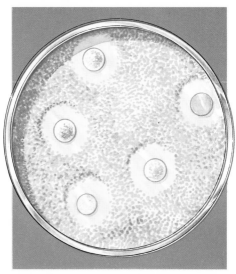

Above: Antibiotic discs prevent the growth of bacterial colonies around them when placed on agar plates. Different antibiotics vary in effect.

type of *Penicillium*. The chemical causing the effect was extracted and Fleming called it penicillin. But because of various problems, penicillin was not produced on a large scale until 1943. However, this drug saved thousands of lives during World War II when it was used to treat many wounded soldiers who were suffering from infections caused by bacteria.

The production of antibiotics
In the early days antibiotics were produced by growing fungi as surface colonies in broad-bottomed flasks, shallow pans or even milk bottles, all of which needed to be thoroughly cleaned or sterilized. Also, only small amounts of antibiotic were produced.

To increase the yields of penicillin, a method was developed for growing the mould in liquid culture in larger vessels. To further increase the amount of penicillin produced, experiments with X-rays and ultra-violet light were carried out. These forms of radiation caused changes in the *Penicillium*, producing new types or mutants which gave higher yields of penicillin. Repeated

Below: The rod-shaped bacteria *Escherichia coli* before exposure to antibiotic.

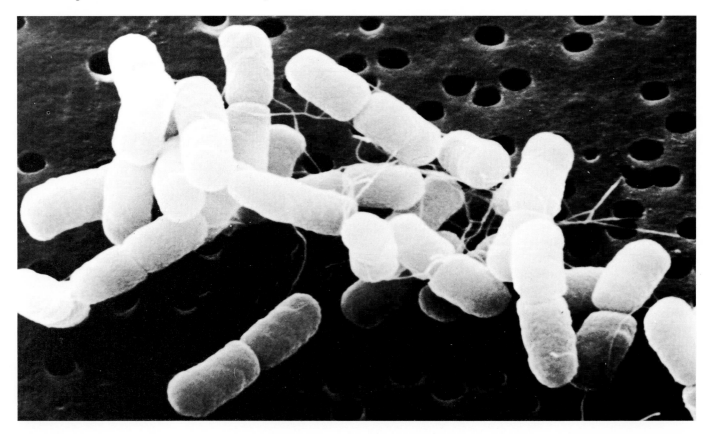

mutation experiments have resulted in even more productive *Penicillium*.

Similar techniques have been used on other antibiotic-producing microbes to increase yield. Modern antibiotic production is carried out using the high-yielding strains in submerged liquid culture.

The use of antibiotics

Penicillin and streptomycin are two antibiotics presently in major use. Penicillin was at first thought to be a wonder-drug which would cure all diseases. But one disease it could not cure was tuberculosis. Since the early 1950s streptomycin has been available to cure tuberculosis and together with vaccination this has resulted in the disease being almost eradicated.

Unfortunately, the increased use of antibiotics has led to the appearance of antibiotic-resistant strains of bacteria. In recent years antibiotics have been widely used to treat relatively minor conditions such as sore throats. Also antibiotics have been used in agriculture to promote growth in animals. This has led to the appearance of some strains of bacteria which survive attack by antibiotics. These new strains cause diseases which are then difficult to cure. One solution to this problem is to discover new types of antibiotics.

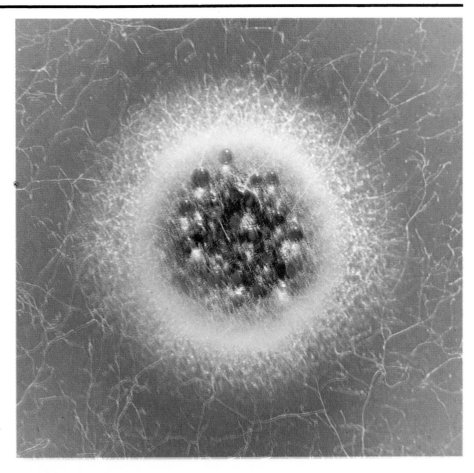

Below: *Escherichia coli* after exposure to antibiotic. The cells have been destroyed as can be seen from the remains.

Above: The fungus *Penicillium* growing on an agar plate. The fine white hyphae are clearly visible as they spread outwards.

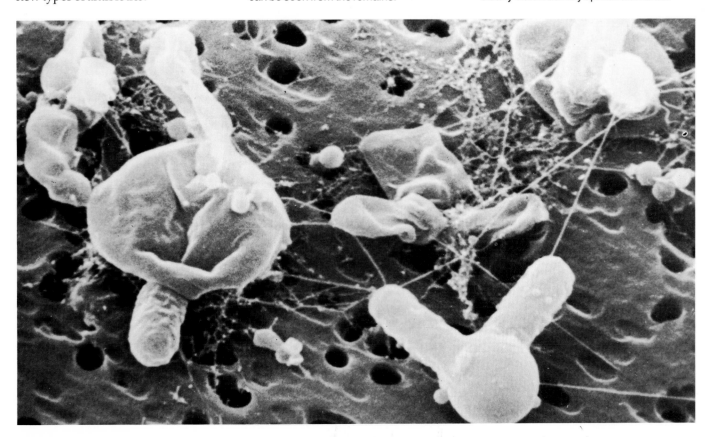

Making new microbes

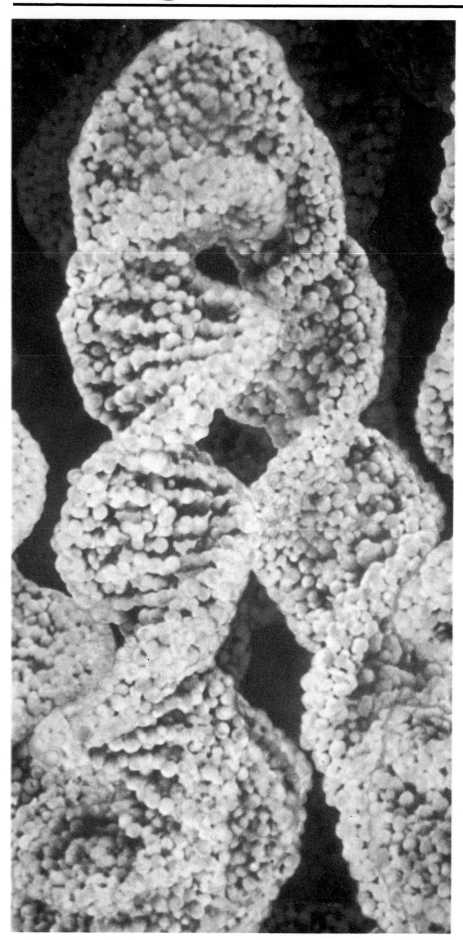

Life on earth is continuously changing. The living organisms of today are different to those which existed millions of years ago. Evolution has occurred. This means that over a long period of time, organisms have changed gradually to form new types. Those types of organisms which cannot adapt die out and become extinct. Only the fittest survive to produce offspring. This is a process of natural selection for the most successful organisms which is called 'survival of the fittest'. It is a simple way of explaining how evolution has occurred naturally.

Since humans have existed on Earth, they have used techniques which artificially speed up the process of evolution. Ever since people started farming, they have been involved in improving breeds of animals and plants. This process is called artificial selection. One example of this is selecting high yielding types of fungi for antibiotic production.

The science of breeding

Breeding results in the production of offspring, but it is basically about passing on characteristics from one generation to another. These characteristics are controlled by genes and the study of inheritance is called genetics. You are similar in many ways to your parents, because you have inherited genes from both your parents. Genes are made of a complex substance called DNA and are found in all living cells making up structures called chromosomes.

The DNA making up the genes controls what living things look like, how they behave and what chemicals, such as enzymes, they can produce. Genes are arranged along the chromosomes just like beads on a necklace. Each gene is responsible for controlling just one character. But, of course, environment also influences living things. For example, a person may inherit genes to make him or her tall but without a proper food supply the person may not actually grow tall.

Bacteria have about 4000 genes, whereas humans have about 5 million genes. In recent years scientists have developed new techniques that have enabled them to isolate and remove genes from one organism and then place

Left: The spiral structure of DNA magnified thousands of times. It is made up of many different molecules which form a double strand with cross-links, like a twisted rope ladder.

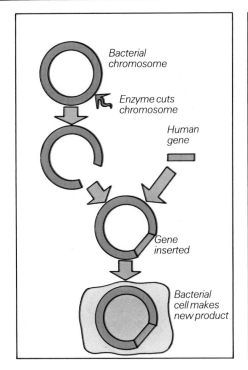

Above: The process of insertion of a human gene into a bacterial chromosome. Once the two are combined, the bacterial cell can make a new product.

Genetic engineering

Since the early 1970s a number of techniques for genetic engineering have been developed. All of the techniques have basic similarities and usually involve taking a gene from a human cell and placing it into a cell of a microbe. Bacteria or fungal cells are commonly used to receive the gene from the human donor cell.

First the required gene must be identified and located on the human chromosome. Once this is done special enzymes are used to cut the gene from the chromosome. In a similar way you could cut a bead from a necklace using scissors. The enzymes work as chemical 'scissors' cutting out the bead-like gene from the DNA of a chromosome. Then the chromosome of the microbial cell must be cut. The human gene, using

Right: Some people think that genetic engineering could produce monsters! However, genetic engineers observe many safety regulations and would never produce anything like this creature.

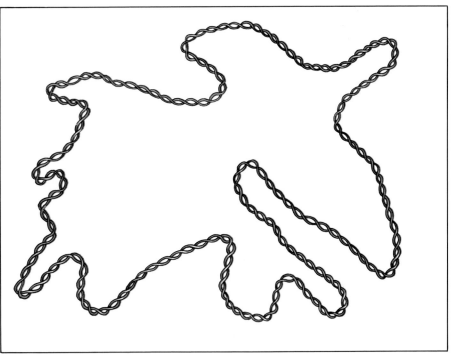

Above: The bacterial chromosome seen in more detail. Groups of molecules along the spiral DNA make up genes which control the many cell processes.

other special enzymes, is then inserted into the microbial cell.

Once inside the cell of the microbe the human gene behaves just as if it were in its own cell and causes the microbe to produce a given product. This new microbial cell is encouraged to reproduce quickly so that lots of this product can be made in a short time. Before genetic engineering was carried out on it, the microbe could not make this particular product controlled by the inserted gene. It can be said that a new microbe is made by this process.

This type of microbe did not exist in nature before. Genetic engineering therefore enables scientists to take pieces of genetic material from different types of organisms and put them together in ways that did not occur naturally. It is a very complex method of artificial selection.

Some products are now being made commercially by means of genetic engineering techniques. Most of those made so far are medically important products that previously could only be obtained by processes involving large quantities of starting material and producing just a few grams of product. New microbes have been artificially made by humans to make products which are useful to humans.

them in another organism. These genes still work inside the new organism producing their own particular products. This process is called genetic manipulation or genetic engineering.

Using new microbes

DNA in the cells of all living things stores the genetic information. When cells divide this information is passed on to the offspring who are able to interpret the code to make proteins, including enzymes, and other cell components. Genetic engineering results in the introduction of new information.

If the new gene is correctly inserted into the cell of a microbe then the microbe will produce a new product such as human insulin. The microbes are then encouraged to divide very quickly by being given ideal conditions when they have a supply of water, food and warmth. The microbes then act as mini-chemical factories, producing large quantities of useful products quickly.

Insulin

Human insulin was the first product of benefit to human health to be made on a commercial scale by recent genetic engineering techniques.

Insulin is a hormone which is made in the pancreas – a gland in the abdomen. Hormones are special proteins which control the activity of the body and insulin regulates the sugar level in our blood. If people do not produce enough insulin they cannot control the blood sugar level, and they suffer from a condition known as diabetes which can result in coma if not controlled. Diabetics are treated by having a carefully controlled diet and/or injections of insulin.

Insulin has been available to treat diabetics for many years, but it is made by extraction and purification from pancreas glands of pigs and cattle. Such insulin is slightly different to human insulin, however, so has to be treated to make it usable by humans. The proportion of diabetics in the world population is getting bigger so it is quite possible that insulin produced from cattle or pigs could not meet the demand of an increased number of diabetics.

The successful production of human insulin by bacteria using genetic engineering techniques was announced in 1978, and such insulin has been available since 1983. As a result of this, diabetics throughout the world have a readily available supply of insulin for their injections. One remaining problem is cost, because insulin production from animals is still much cheaper than production by microbes. But scientific research in one area often results in many new discoveries, and it may be possible to make human insulin from pig insulin by using new enzyme techniques to change the pig insulin.

Human growth hormone

A number of other medicines are still scarce and expensive because they can only be made from materials such as human organs which are in limited supply. One example is human growth hormone. Some children have too little of this so that their growth is stunted and they become dwarfs. This condition can be treated by injections of the growth hormone which can be made from extracts of human thyroid gland. (The thyroid gland is in the neck and produces a hormone which controls normal

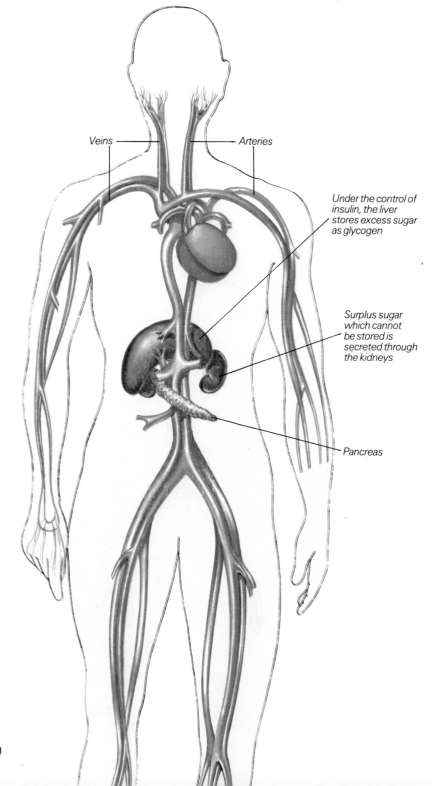

Left: Insulin is produced in the pancreas and regulates blood sugar levels throughout the body's circulatory system.

Veins

Arteries

Under the control of insulin, the liver stores excess sugar as glycogen

Surplus sugar which cannot be stored is secreted through the kidneys

Pancreas

Interferon

Interferon is a chemical produced in very tiny quantities by human cells. It is thought to play a natural part in defence against disease, especially attack by viruses. Since people believe that some types of cancer may be caused by viruses, the discovery of interferon was welcomed in the medical world as a possible cure for cancer. One of the problems in even investigating this, however, was the short supply and therefore very high expense of interferon. This has made it very difficult to carry out suitable experiments. Recent work with genetic engineering techniques have resulted in the successful production, in fairly large quantities, of interferon from yeast cells. This will mean that necessary research, using this drug, can be carried out to find if it really can successfully treat cancer.

Left: The man holding the football is a dwarf who is manager of an Italian football team. If growth hormone had been available when he was a child, he could have grown normally.

Below: These human cells have been grown in a laboratory. They are used to manufacture antibodies using techniques developed in research on microbes.

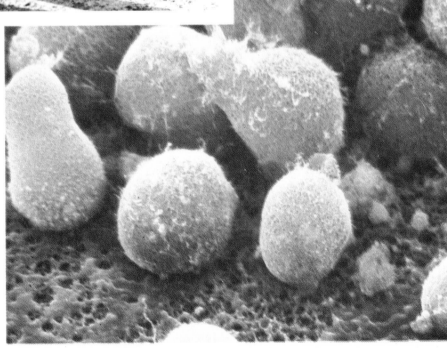

growth.) But the availability of thyroid glands from human corpses is small, and so there is always a limited supply of growth hormone. Only one out of six children who need it can be treated.

One growth hormone has been produced from other animals but this is a very complex process. Only 0.005 grams of pure hormone were obtained from half a million sheep brains! This amount of hormone could be extracted from 9 litres of bacteria.

Much work is being carried out on genetic engineering techniques in an attempt to 'persuade' microbes to produce this hormone artificially. Supplies from this new source are expected to be on the market by 1985 and will mean that all dwarf children can be treated. Enough hormone will also be available for other purposes, such as the treatment of people's broken bones.

Will microbes change our life?

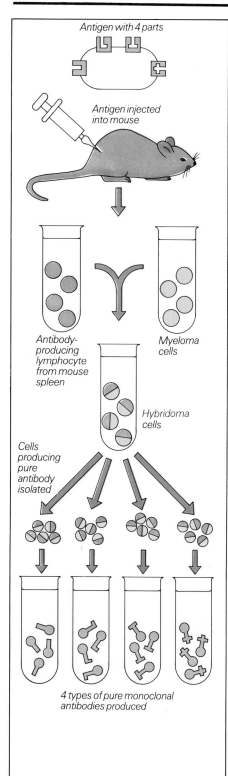

Antigen with 4 parts

Antigen injected into mouse

Antibody-producing lymphocyte from mouse spleen

Myeloma cells

Hybridoma cells

Cells producing pure antibody isolated

4 types of pure monoclonal antibodies produced

Above: The production of monoclonal antibodies by using microbial antigens. Hybridoma cells are produced and these can manufacture very pure antibodies which may result in many new benefits to our health.

It has been said "Never underestimate the power of the microbe"! Microbes will almost certainly have a dramatic effect on our lives. Recent scientific advances, using microbes, could improve health, food production, agriculture, the environment and energy production.

Problems

But many people are concerned about the possible risk of using microbes. Of course, one of the most obvious risks is that governments will decide to use genetic engineering to produce microbes which will cause terrible new diseases, and use them as a weapon of war. However, this risk can be reduced by agreements between countries not to do this. But there is still the risk that such new diseases could arise accidentally during genetic engineering for some other purpose. During the 1970s this became such a cause of worry that the scientists who were carrying out the first experiments in genetic engineering on microbes called a halt on work for some time until they agreed on safety precautions that must be taken in laboratories carrying out genetic engineering.

There are other risks, some of which have already been mentioned, of using new products, such as sensitivity to washing powders containing enzymes and microbes becoming resistant to antibiotics through over-use. These problems, too, can be solved, for example by producing different types of antibiotics. But it is always possible for new side-effects to occur in the future and so scientists have to test products very thoroughly for safety.

Another problem is that with the improvements in health due to microbial products, the world's population will increase even more, causing greater demand on food supplies which are already insufficient. Although microbial food production seems to provide a solution, it is unlikely that the developing countries which suffer most from food shortage will be able to afford to use such methods. Their main hope must lie in the development of improved methods of farming and better crops, such as wheat or rice which carry nitrogen-fixing bacteria in their roots.

So although microbes can give us many benefits now and in the future, these organisms need to be treated with great care and caution.

Benefits to health

Many drugs which were previously not

Above: Using bacteria to extract metals from waste ore around a mine. This process is known as bacterial leaching. Certain bacteria live on the waste, producing metal compounds which can be washed out.

available or in short supply will soon be made by microbes. Manufacture of insulin and human growth hormone by bacteria and interferon by yeasts has already been described. Another area which may have great benefits is the manufacture of monoclonal antibodies.

Under normal circumstances when a person becomes infected with a disease-causing microbe, antibodies are produced which react against the microbe. A specific antibody is produced to react with a particular part of an antigen. So several types of antibody are produced, each one by particular white blood cells. Now, using recently developed techniques, these particular blood cells can join or fuse with myeloma cells which are cells that can be grown outside a living organism, in the laboratory.

These fused cells, called hybridoma cells, can therefore produce very pure antibodies which obviously means purer vaccines. These monoclonal antibodies also open up many other possibilities for ways of treating disease.

The environment
Certain microbes can live on metal ores. As they do so they convert the metal ores and release valuable metals such as copper or gold. Microbes are now being used to mine metals. This new method of mining can be carried out in areas which were previously inaccessible to conventional methods of mining. Microbes can also be used to extract more metal from waste left over from the usual methods of mining.

Many useful products can be made by the chemical industry. However, pollutants such as smoke or dirty water are often released from these factories. Microbes can be used in one of two ways to reduce pollution. Either they can feed and grow on the wastes from chemical factories and convert these wastes into useful products or they can replace the chemical factories and make the products themselves without any pollution.

Energy
Oil is a major source of energy. At present much of the oil in oil wells is not obtainable by the techniques in use and this means that valuable oil remains in the ground. It may soon be possible to pump certain microbes into oil wells so that much more of the valuable oil can be reclaimed as the microbes separate the oil from impurities. Microbes are already adding to the world's available fuel by their involvement in gasohol production and this may become more common, providing a renewable source of fuel.

In such ways, microbes can be our invisible allies. They are already used to make many useful products. They will be used to make more products in the future. Modern research techniques, with microbes being used as miniature factories, mean that microbes *can* change our life.

Left: Vaccines are produced from the microbes which cause disease. Vaccination protects against diseases and can bring great benefits to health, particularly in babies who have not yet developed natural immunity.

A-Z Glossary

Aerobic respiration is a type of respiration in which foods are completely broken down in the presence of oxygen to release energy, with carbon dioxide and water as waste products.

Agar is a carbohydrate extracted from seaweeds and used as a nutrient for microbial growth.

Algae are a group of small plants whose bodies vary from microscopic single cells to large seaweeds.

Alimentary canal is the part of animals' bodies where foods are broken down into simpler substances.

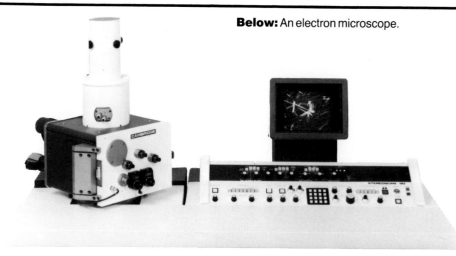

Below: An electron microscope.

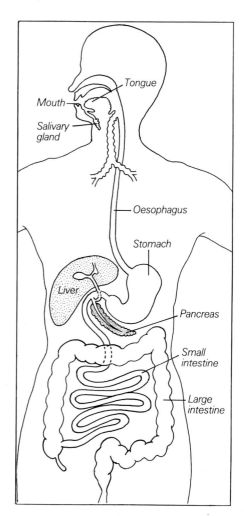

Above: The alimentary canal.

Amino acids are organic compounds which combine in large numbers to make up proteins. Combinations of some of 20 amino acids are commonly found in proteins.

Anaerobic respiration is cellular respiration without oxygen. Chemical energy is released from food by a series of reactions. In animal and plant cells and in some microbes glucose is broken down to lactic acid. Alcohol may be produced by some plants and microbes. The word fermentation is sometimes used instead of anaerobic respiration.

Antibiotics are chemicals that are made by certain microbes and limit or kill the growth of other microbes.

Antibody is a protein made by an animal in response to attack by microbes. It results in an immune response to further attack by that type of microbe.

Antigen is a part of a microbe that stimulates an animal to make a certain type of antibody.

Asexual reproduction is any form of reproduction in which new individuals are derived from a single parent.

Autotrophic organisms (autotrophs) can make their own food from simple starting materials. Green plants are autotrophs.

Bacteria are single-celled microbes. They have a rigid cell wall. They reproduce by dividing to form two new cells.

Carbohydrates are an important group of compounds consisting of carbon, hydrogen and oxygen.

Catalyst is a substance which speeds up a chemical or physical reaction. The catalysts in biological systems are enzymes.

Cell is the basic unit of all living things. Cells are surrounded by a cell membrane and contain cytoplasm. Cells also contain genetic material (DNA), which controls inheritance, in chromosomes.

Cell division is the process by which a cell divides into two.

Chromosome is one of a number of thread-like structures that occur within the nucleus of a cell and constitute the genetic material of the cell. Chromosomes contain DNA.

Cytoplasm is the living content of a cell.

Decomposer is an organism which feeds on dead organic matter and breaks it down into simple materials.

Digestion is the process of breaking down complex foods into simple molecules that can be absorbed and used by the body tissues.

DNA (deoxyribonucleic acid) is the major constituent of the chromosomes and is the hereditary material of most living things.

Electron microscope is a microscope which uses electrons to produce magnified images of objects.

Enzyme is a special type of protein that speeds up reactions inside living cells.

Evolution is the gradual change of living organisms from ancestral types as time passes.

Excretion is the elimination by an organism of its waste products.

Faeces are the solid remains of undigested food and other wastes.

Fermentation is the process of using food to release energy without the use of oxygen. Alcoholic fermentation is carried out by certain yeasts and bacteria. Glucose is converted into alcohol. A common product of fermentation in animal cells is lactic acid.

Fertilization is the fusion of two special sex cells to form a new cell. It is the essential characteristic of sexual reproduction.

Fungi are a group of plants which typically form a mycelium (mass of threads). Fungi lack chlorophyll and cannot make their own food.

Gene is one of the basic units of heredity. Genes are found on chromosomes.

Genetic engineering is the deliberate alteration of the structure of chromosomes by artificial means.

Genetics is the branch of biology concerned with the study of heredity.

Glucose is a simple sugar.

Hormones are chemical substances involved in the control of the activities occurring within our bodies.

Hypha is one of the strands that form the bodies of most fungi.

Immunity is the ability of an animal or plant to resist and/or overcome infection.

Immunization is the process of making an animal resistant to infection.

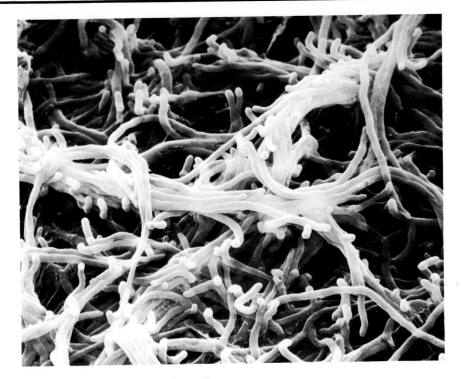

Above: The hyphae of a fungal mycelium.

Infection is the process of invasion of an organism or part of an organism by disease-causing microbes.

Insulin is a protein hormone which controls blood sugar levels and is made in the pancreas.

Interferons are proteins made by animal cells in response to infection by viruses. They play a part in the recovery from viral infection.

Lactic acid is an acid produced during the breakdown of glucose in animal cells and in certain microbes.

Micrometre (symbol μm) is a microscopic unit of distance equal to one thousandth of a millimetre. Many bacteria are about 1 μm across.

Microscope is an instrument used to magnify material to show structures invisible to the naked eye. The light microscope uses light to give a magnified image of the specimen. The usual type is a compound microscope, that is, one that has two convex lenses that combine to give high magnification. The best light microscope magnifies about 1500 times. The electron microscope uses electrons to give a magnified image. It can magnify up to one million times.

Mutation is a change in the DNA structure of the chromosomes.

Mycelium is the mass of threads or hyphae which form a fungus. Fruiting bodies such as toadstools grow from the mycelium.

Mycorrhizae are the association between fungal hyphae and the roots of higher plants.

Natural selection is one of the processes involved in evolution.

Nitrification is the process by which some bacteria in the soil convert nitrogen-containing compounds into nitrates, which can be absorbed easily by plants.

Nitrogen cycle is the circulation of nitrogen and its compounds in nature. The cycle involves the activities of nitrogen-fixing microbes which convert free nitrogen to nitrates and the action of nitrifying bacteria. Some of the nitrates are used by plants in protein synthesis.

Nitrogen fixation is the incorporation of gaseous nitrogen into compounds containing nitrogen. In nature this is brought about by some bacteria in the soil or bacteria in the root nodules of legumes.

Nutritional requirements are the essential food supply necessary for the growth and maintenance of an organism.

Parasite is an organism that lives in or on another living organism (the host) from which it obtains food, shelter and other requirements. The host may be damaged by the activity of the parasite.

Pasteurization is a process of heat treatment that reduces the number of harmful microbes in foods and drinks, for example milk.

Phagocyte is a cell that engulfs other cells.

Photosynthesis is the process by which green plants and some microbes make their own food using sunlight as a source of energy.

Pollution is the presence in the environment of substances at a level that causes undesirable effects.

Protein is one of the chemicals that are fundamental to the structure and function of all living cells. Proteins are made up of chains of amino acids.

Protozoa are a group of microscopic animals (also called protozoans).

Respiration is a process which occurs in all living cells to release energy from food.

Rusts are a group of parasitic fungi which attack plants of agricultural importance, for example, cereals.

Saprophyte is an organism that obtains its nourishment from dead or decaying matter. Many fungi and bacteria are saprophytes; they play an important part in the recycling of nutrients.

Septic tank is where raw sewage is piped and stored for gradual decomposition by microbes.

Sewage is waste from animals or humans consisting of water, urine, faeces and other unwanted material.

Sexual reproduction is any form of reproduction in which two sex cells or gametes join to produce a new cell, which develops into a new organism.

Solution is formed when a solid material is dissolved in a liquid.

Species is a group of organisms that interbreed with each other to produce fertile offspring.

Sugar is any carbohydrate that has a sweet taste and is soluble in water.

Symbiosis is any close relationship between two different types of living organism where both benefit.

Vaccination is the giving of a vaccine, usually by an injection, which results in immunity.

Virus is a minute infectious agent. Viruses can only survive and reproduce inside other living cells.

Vitamin is an organic substance required in small quantities for good health because they are necessary for many of the activities of living things.

Yeasts are a group of fungi. Yeasts are used in bread and beer making.

Reference

History, people and events

The history of work with microbes is related to three important issues. Firstly, microbes provided food and drink for more than 8000 years before they were discovered in the seventeenth century. This meant that people had been using microbes to make useful products for many years without realising it.

Secondly, until the nineteenth century many people believed in the *'Theory of Spontaneous Generation'*. The basic idea of spontaneous generation was that life can arise from non-living things very quickly. If food is allowed to stand for some time it decays. When it is examined with a microscope it is found to contain many microbes. Where do these microbes come from since they are not seen in fresh food? We now know that microbes settle from the air on to food where they grow and multiply, so causing decay.

Thirdly, what causes contagious disease? Before the nineteenth century people did not realise that some microbes cause disease.

Microbiology is the study of microbes and it did not develop until the latter part of the nineteenth century. By that time microscopes had been developed, techniques for studying microbes had been devised and the relationship between microbes and the three important issues already mentioned had been made clear.

Here are some of the important events, with people involved with them, during the history of work with microbes from very early times until the present:-

Before 6000BC. The Sumerians and Babylonians used yeast to make alcohol.
About 4000 BC. The Egyptians used yeast to make bread.
About 350 BC. Aristotle played an important part in developing the 'Theory of Spontaneous Generation'. According to him some animals came from dew falling on leaves, others from decaying mud, dung or timber. Fleas, bugs and lice were supposed to be produced from moisture and filth, and it was even believed that some fish arise from mud, sand or decayed matter.
By the fourteenth century AD the distillation of alcohol (spirits) from fermented grain was common in many parts of the world.
Other ancient processes using microbes:-
Cultivation of acetic acid bacteria to make vinegar.
Cultivation of lactic acid bacteria to preserve milk in the form of yoghurt.
Cultivation of various bacteria and moulds to produce cheese.

1664. Robert Hooke described the fruiting structures of moulds.
1668. Redi, an Italian physician, investigated the spontaneous generation of

Above: Anton van Leeuwenhoek's microscope looks very different from modern microscopes.

Below: Van Leeuwenhoek's drawing of yeast cells viewed through his microscope.

maggots from meat. He proceeded to disprove this theory by covering one portion of meat with muslin, whereas another portion of the same meat was left uncovered. Maggots only developed on the uncovered meat. Adult flies laid eggs which developed into maggots on the uncovered meat. The muslin prevented the eggs from contaminating the other meat. Redi's work was not generally accepted at the time and it was not for another 200 years that the theory of spontaneous generation was finally disproved.
1684. Anton van Leeuwenhoek discovered 'animalcules'. We now call them microbes. He was able to see them by using the microscope which he developed.
1776. Spallanzani, an Italian scientist, developed techniques for sterilizing broth and equipment so that microbes would not grow. He worked with liquids or infusions made from seeds or vegetables and found many microbes growing in these liquids. By boiling the infusions and sterilizing any air in contact with them he was able to show that microbes would not appear.
1836. Schwann, a German scientist, passed heated air into boiled nutrient medium and stopped the growth of microbes.
1853. Schroeder filtered air before allowing it to circulate in a sterilized container containing boiled broth. Again the growth of microbes was not observed.
1861. Louis Pasteur of France finally disproved the theory of spontaneous

generation by simple experiments he had devised. He designed a swan-necked flask in which liquid broth was present. He then boiled the broth and the vapour produced forced the air from the neck of the flask and out into the atmosphere. When the broth cooled the air inside the flask contracted so causing air from the atmosphere to enter. However, dust and microbes in this air become trapped in the bend of the 'S' shaped neck.

This is because dust and microbes are slightly heavier than air and settle under gravity. The result was that no microbes grew in the broth, which was therefore sterile. Only when a flask treated in a similar way was tilted so that the dust and microbes in the neck mixed with the broth did the broth become colonized by microbes.

Pasteur later improved sterilization techniques which led to Pasteurization of liquids such as milk. This technique involved heating and rapidly cooling a liquid so that most microbes in it are killed, and is still used nowadays to produce 'Pasteurized milk'. Pasteur also did much work on fermentation in microbes. He also carried out work using different types of microbes and watching how they interacted. He thought that microbes may be used as agents to cure infections. This prediction came true about 50 years later when penicillin was discovered.
1876. Robert Koch was able to show that some microbes caused disease. In fact the first clear demonstration that microbes

cause disease had been by M.J. Berkeley in 1845, who showed that a mould was responsible for Irish Potato Blight. It was the work of Koch, however, which confirmed beyond doubt the link between microbes and contagious disease.

In his early work Koch studied anthrax, a disease of cattle, which sometimes also occurs in man. Anthrax is caused by bacteria and the blood of an animal infected with anthrax has many of these bacteria present. Koch established by careful use of microscopes that the bacteria were always present in the blood of an animal that had the disease. When he took a small sample of this blood and injected it into another animal, it in turn became diseased and died. He repeated this many times to show that the bacteria in the blood were causing disease.

He also found that the bacteria could be grown in liquids outside the animal's body. Bacteria from a diseased animal and bacteria in culture both caused the same disease when re-inoculated into an animal. He was later able to show that a certain type of bacteria causes a certain type of disease.

Koch also devised a technique called pure culture for growing bacteria. These are growths of one type of bacteria only. He worked out how to obtain these from mixed cultures containing many different types of bacteria. This meant that a given type could be grown and studied.

1884. Hans Gram, a Dane, devised a technique using a staining solution which distinguishes between two major groups of bacteria. Some are 'gram positive' and some 'gram negative'. Members of each group have certain things in common, but differ from members of the other group.

1885. Joseph Lister, an English surgeon and scientist, developed antiseptic treatment of wounds during and after surgery. He used special chemicals which prevented microbes from entering wounds and causing infection and thus increased the chances of the patients surviving.

1897. Eduard Buchner of Germany found that an extract of macerated (squashed) yeast, freed of whole cells by filtration, retained the ability to convert sugar into alcohol. His discovery gave rise to the field of biochemistry. This is the study of the chemistry of living systems. Nowadays biochemists often work with microbes and their enzymes.

1900. Paul Ehrlich carried out important work with microbes and immunity.

1928. Alexander Fleming discovered penicillin. During the 50 years after the work of Pasteur various microbial preparations were tried as medicines but they were either too poisonous or too inactive in live animals. In 1928 Fleming noted that a mould killed his bacterial cultures. He grew the mould in a liquid broth and separated fluid from the mould cells. He found that this cell-free fluid stopped the growth of many kinds of bacteria. He called the active ingredient in the liquid penicillin but did no further work on it. Penicillin was later to be called a 'wonder drug' as it cured many diseases.

1941. Howard Florey and E. Chain were able to isolate and grow large quantities of penicillin. After the work of Fleming many scientists found that penicillin would not keep. Florey used a mould related to that used by Fleming to produce large quantities of a form of penicillin which did not lose its effectiveness. This began the production of antibiotics as drugs.

During the 1940s. Selman Waksman, of the USA, succeeded in obtaining a number of new antibiotics from soil microbes. The best known of these is streptomycin.

1952. Crick and Watson discovered the structure of DNA. This was a major breakthrough in the study of genetics since genetic information is stored in DNA. Since that time microbes, because they breed quickly, have been used to study inheritance.

1973 The first experiments using genetic engineering techniques were carried out. These techniques are now being used to make either new products from microbes or to produce materials which were previously available, but perhaps only in small quantities.

Books to read

Microbes in Your Life by Leo Schneider, published by Harcourt, Brace, Jovanovich.

Microbes and Us by Hugh Nichol, published by R. West.

Magnificent Microbes by Bernard Dixon, published by Atheneum.

Bacteria: How They Affect Other Living Things by Dorothy H. Patent, published by Holiday.

Introduction to Biology by D.G. MacKean, published by International Ideas.

Acknowledgements

Photographs
Pete Addis: 23
Aldus Archive: 19T, 30B
Beecham Pharmaceuticals: 6, 7, 36, 37B, 44
Biofotos: 8TR & BR, 10, 29L, 30T, 33, 37T
Paul Brierley: cover, 5T & B
British Charcoal & Macdonalds: 24T
Cambridge Instruments Ltd.: 45
Bruce Coleman Ltd: 29R
Glaxo Holdings plc: 17
Alan Hutchison Library: 24B
Kennecott: 42-43
Long Ashton Research Station: 8BL
Mansell Collection: 26L, 32, 35L & R, 46
Milk Marketing Board: 13T
Oxfam: 31T; 43B
Rex Features: 41
G.R. Roberts: 26R
Rowntree Mackintosh plc: 22
Royal Society: 46
Science Photo Library: 8TL, 13B, 14, 21, 41
Scientific American Books: 38 (From "Powers of Ten" by Philip Morrison and Phylis Morrison & the office of Charles and Ray Eames © 1982)
Whitbread & Co.: 18L & C, 19BL
ZEFA: title page, 18BR, 19BR, 31B

Artists
Ann Baum, Gerard Browne, Bill le Fever, Jeremy Gower, Michael Robinson, Annie Russell

Index

1 2 3 4 5 6 7 8-U-88 87 86 85 84